DESIGNER CLOTHES TO MAKE

Charmian Watkins
DESIGNER CLOTHES
TO MAKE

COLLINS

First published in 1985 by William Collins Sons & Co Ltd
London · Glasgow · Sydney · Auckland · Toronto · Johannesburg

British Library Cataloguing in Publication Data
Watkins, Charmian
Designer Clothes to Make
I. Dressmaking
I. Title
646.4'04   TT515

ISBN 0-00-411741-7

Typeset by Text Typesetters, London
Colour separations by Culver Graphics, High Wycombe
Printed and bound by William Collins, Glasgow

C O N T E N T S

Introduction   6
General Notes   8

Fine and Dandy   10
Patterns   20

Sports Chic   28
Patterns   38

Country House   44
Patterns   55

Summer Breeze   64
Patterns   76

Streets Ahead   82
Patterns   92

Holiday Snaps   98
Patterns   111

After Dark   116
Patterns   128

Permutations   136
Credits   144

INTRODUCTION

I believe that everyone should have the sort of clothes that make them feel confident, relaxed and happy. Clothing is essential to us all. It is an everyday fact of life, and bearing in mind today's prices for well-made and thought-out garments, it really makes sense to make your own.

This book is therefore designed and written for all of you who appreciate and long for good designer clothes, which exhibit strong style and interesting cut, and who for one reason or another choose to make rather than buy them. The designs include clothes suitable for ages 17-70, and their styling ranges from the relaxed and easy-to-make to sophisticated and tailored garments for special dressing that require more time and expertise. I have tried to provide you with all the tools you need to beat the system; by using the book to the full, you can achieve an individual and distinctive wardrobe of designer outfits with relative ease.

It would be wrong to claim this book is for the complete beginner, but if you can use the straight stitch button on your machine, you will be able to begin with one of the simpler designs, say a straight skirt or the little evening top. In this way you will soon gain an understanding of the making up process and so increase confidence, enabling you to move on to tackling garments that require more work and know-how.

I have tried to make the book as clear as possible. There are precise, step-by-step instructions, which together with back-up diagrams, will provide you with all you need to make up the clothes successfully. By following my instructions to the letter, even a relative beginner should be able to achieve amazing results. The rules are simple: do as I suggest, in the order given – I have taken great pains to explain clearly the logical order in which a garment should be put together; this way you won't come to grief.

The little diagrams I mentioned are to reinforce even more clearly how a particular process should be approached. The patterns, and their grades, have been carefully thought out for maximum clarity, whilst not losing any of the designer cut which gives these clothes their strong 'handwriting'. And anyone familiar with even a little dressmaking will understand the language and terminology I have used, excepting perhaps 'basting', which is simply the American word for tacking.

I have also included some of my sketch-book drawings to show my original ideas. They may be rough, but I find that cutting patterns directly from these ensures that the finished garments lose nothing in their translation; they work out exactly as envisaged. I thought it would be interesting for you to see the full process, from first thought to final product. These sketches also fulfil a secondary function: they set the mood of each outfit. The photography takes this one step further by adding 'gloss', and emphasizing the character of the clothes. You will find both 'mood' shots and pictures of each individual garment in as many combinations as I could think of. These will not only help you to see just how a jacket looks with a skirt as compared to the same jacket with a pair of pants, but hopefully will encourage you to experiment.

The fabrics I have chosen range from wool and cotton to linen and silk satin. All the coordination and detailing have been carefully thought out so that far from looking homemade, the completed garments all display the finely finished detail that sends the cost of similar ready-made clothes rocketing sky high in the shops.

The clothes have been grouped into outfits. A list of exactly what you need to make them up is given, followed by instructions and diagrams, and finally their patterns, drawn one-fifth of their full size. There is a separate section at the back of the book called 'Permutations', and this offers alternative fabric suggestions should you choose to create a totally different look. In addition, many of the clothes are interchangeable and can be made up in winter or summer fabrics.

We all want to make successfully finished clothes to wear and enjoy rather than end up with a pile of half-finished catastrophes in the cupboard, so please cast your eye over the list of hints and tips given overleaf on pages 8–9. All specific details are given within each set of individual instructions, but by following the advice given, you can minimize time and effort, and reduce the risk of disaster.

I hope you have as much fun using the book as I have had in writing it.

The author with her favourite Singer sewing machine.

Size 10

bust	83cm
waist	61cm
hips	89cm

Size 12

bust	88cm
waist	66cm
hips	94cm

Size 14

bust	93cm
waist	71cm
hips	99cm

Key to Patterns

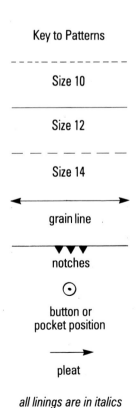

- - - - - - - - - -

Size 10

─────────────

Size 12

─ ─ ─ ─ ─ ─ ─

Size 14

◄─────────►

grain line

▼ ▼ ▼

notches

⊙

button or
pocket position

────►

pleat

all linings are in italics

It is important to read the following hints and tips before starting to make any of the clothes in this book.

Sizing

The reason I have only included three sizes of patterns – 10, 12 and 14 – is that additional lines would have made the grading difficult to follow. I have tried to make the grades I have used as simple as possible to 'read' and you should be able to draw up the patterns very easily. If you are smaller than a size 10 or larger than a size 14, as many of us are, you can compare your measurements to those on the chart shown left and adjust the sizing as necessary, making sure the pattern pieces will still fit together.

Drawing up the patterns

Each little square on your pattern represents a one centimetre square. Having chosen the sizing you wish to follow, and using pattern paper marked out in one centimetre squares, transfer the lines on your page onto the pattern paper. I would suggest starting at the top right-hand point of each pattern piece, and marking every two or three squares, drawing little crosses at each point round your pattern, to finish where you began. Any mistakes should be self-evident since the drawing will not finish at the starting point. Straight lines need only be marked with a cross at top and bottom, to save time. Now work around your pattern piece once more, adding all notch marks and any other instructions, and marking in the grainline of each piece. Seam allowances of 1·5cm have been included on all the pattern pieces except where otherwise indicated. Finally, cut your pattern out.

Laying out the pattern

Most patterns can be cut on the fold, thus ensuring a pair, for example, of sleeves rather than two left sleeves. Set out your fabric on the fold, right sides inside. I suggest always placing the 'head' or top of each pattern piece in one direction only. I usually cut out on the kitchen table, with the 'heads' of my pattern pieces facing towards the garden. This is simply a safety precaution for one-way fabrics – one-way grains etc. It is so easy to forget that a check, for instance, will only work one way – indeed you may not notice at all until it becomes horribly self-evident when worn.

Lays (or fabric quantities) have been given for each individual garment. If you choose to use a fabric of a different width, before investing in it, lay out your pattern exactly as described, firstly marking the table or floor with rulers or tape measures to set out the perimeters of your chosen cloth when folded in half lengthways. This will show you how much fabric is required. Do remember though to add extra fabric for checks and patterns, since these may have to be matched, and in the case of a large check, could account for an extra 50cm of material. Either pin patterns into position or mark round each pattern with white chalk, making sure that grainlines of pattern and fabric match. Double-check each piece before commencing to cut.

Fabrics

The fabrics I used to make up the garments for photography were ideal for my purposes. However, it is possible to completely change the look of an outfit by the use of another equally interesting cloth. The 'Permutations' pages given towards the end of the book will give you some ideas. If this is the case, ask yourself some simple questions: will the fabric I have chosen hang well? is it really suitable to the style of the garment? The Country House suit would look totally wrong made up in a cotton lawn, but would take very kindly to a cotton gaberdine; you could omit the lining for summer wear.

Do check which neatening stitches are most suitable for the fabric chosen; different cloths need different treatment. The best answer is always to first test a little off-cut, using the stitch you feel might work best.

I have kept interfacings at a minimum, since I like the character of a cloth to come through in the design. As a general rule, match your interfacing to your fabric, weight for weight, and only use where absolutely necessary, such as in a rever.

When working with silk, remember that it can take twice as long to make up as, for example, a lightweight wool, textured cotton or pure linen; silk is often slippery and surprisingly heavy. Approach it as a living thing. Use a very small zigzag stitch to neaten, being careful not to stretch fabric cut on the cross; instead give the silk a little respect by pulling all loose thread ends to the inside, tying off and threading away to hide them.

The use of jersey should not frighten anyone, but there are two important points to remember: use a ballpoint needle so as not to cut the knit, and a very small zigzag stitch throughout; this will allow the fabric to move without breaking the seams. Instructions for neatening seams have *not* been included since this type of jersey does not fray – neatening would stiffen them.

Preparing to sew

I would strongly advise that when you set up your machine to begin work on any garment, you also set up the iron and board as a matter of course. Pressing throughout the making-up process is of vital importance to the professional finish of your garment, so don't skimp – it takes more time to unpick a pulled seam allowance and reset it than it does to press it flat in the first place. Pressing a sleevehead is best done with a clean tea towel folded into a pad. Hold it inside the sleevehead whilst spraying the curve of the sleevehead with the steam iron, held in your other hand, at a distance of between 10–30cm. Pressing velvet should again be left to a minimum or done at a distance with steam only, as above. There are velvet and sleevehead presses available on the market but since the whole concept of this book is based on saving money rather than spending it, I would suggest the cheaper alternative!

A note on collars

Top collars and undercollars have been cut as one in your patterns for ease of understanding. Adjustments come within the instructions for each individual pattern, where depending on the weight of fabric and the curve of the collar, the undercollar will jut out beneath the top collar since it has less far to roll. It can then be trimmed, as instructed, if this proves necessary.

Sampling

Before you begin sewing, experiment with stitch length, size of needle etc., on a small offcut of fabric. Use a 70's needle for all fine work, such as silk or cotton lawn, moving through an 80's size of needle for medium weights, to a 90's for heavy wool coating. Bearing in mind the notes on working with jersey (described under 'Fabrics'), periodically check the smooth head of your ballpoint needle throughout the sewing process to make sure it is not damaged; blunting will cause dropped stitches and could also damage

the cloth. And never sew over pins, otherwise you will spend a fortune in machine needles.

Pinning and basting

Don't be afraid to pin or baste pattern pieces to set them in place, whichever method you prefer. And always match notches – they are there for a purpose.

Buttonholes

Before attacking a garment, make a sample buttonhole using an offcut of the fabric you propose to use. All patterns are marked with button positions. The rule is to set your button overlapping the button position marked on your garment by 2mm, towards the folded edge of the cloth; make a pin mark. At the other inner side of the button, mark 2mm further in than its inner edge with a second pin. Remove the button and mark across these two pin marks at lines parallel with the folded edge, then using another thread, mark from pin mark to pin mark, at right angles to the folded edge (see Fig.1). The buttonhole is now ready to sew.

Zips

I have given instructions for setting in zips which include the use of stabstitching if sewing by hand. To stabstitch a zip into position, simply insert your needle into the right side of the fabric, 5mm away from the folded zip edge, and come through to the right side again, 5–6mm further down the stitching line. On the right side, work a small backstitch, passing the needle through again to the wrong side and coming up 5–6mm again to the right side, further down the stitching line. Repeat to complete your zip insertion. (See Fig.2.)

Clipping curves and trimming corners

When following instructions for clipping into curves to ease, clip evenly around a curved line down to two to three threads away from the stitching line. Similarly, where trimming is indicated, cut across a corner, about three threads from the stitching line.

Hem and sleeve lengths

Finally, remember to adjust lengths of hem and cuff before finishing off, if necessary. I have cut the lengths according to the style of each garment, but ultimately the choice is yours.

fig.1

BUTTON POSITION

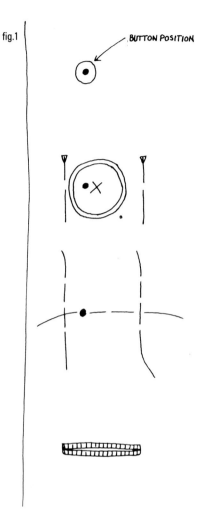

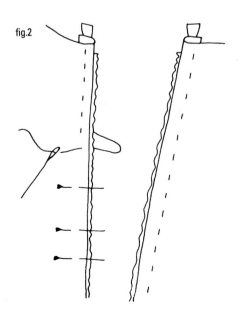

fig.2

This sharply defined outfit is based on eighteenth century hacking and riding styles. It incorporates a strong use of inserts, either in velvet or another contrast fabric, set against a classically conservative material such as the cavalry twill used here. In this instance, an integrated look is achieved by lifting the colour interest with a furnishing fabric moiré. The overall effect is thrown into even stronger perspective by the treatment of one of the garments: the fine silk shirt that buttons at the back leaving the front clear for pleating and machine embroidered detail. A casually tied stock at the neck completes the softening effect. The high-waisted skirt is particularly flattering; the deep flare that cuts into the back – a feature repeated on both the jacket and coat – makes for ease of wear.

Fine & Dandy

YOU WILL NEED

1.40m of 150cm wide fabric (main)
50cm of 120cm wide fabric (contrast 1 – velvet)
50cm of 115cm wide fabric (contrast 2 – moiré)
65cm of 150cm wide lining fabric
65cm of 150cm wide interfacing
10cm of domette
1 large velvet-covered button

fig.1

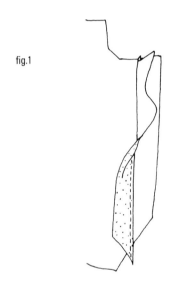

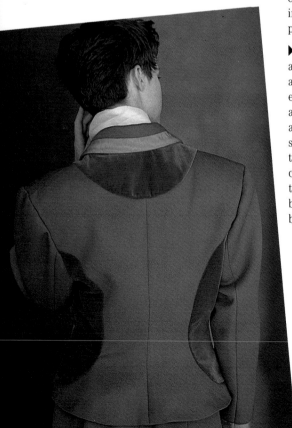

The waisted jacket shown here has a single front button fastening, set in pockets, and shaped interest on both the front and back in the form of contrast inserts. You may omit the extra trim on the collar, revers and on the cuff edges if you wish, but the whole jacket should be lined, as instructed, for style, comfort and ease of wear.

▶1　Attach interfacing to top collar, top cuffs, back neck insert, pockets and front facing pieces.

▶2　To make up back, attach centre back pieces, right sides together and matching notches; stitch and press seam allowances open. Clip seam allowance at centre back waist area to ease, then attach centre back neck insert, matching notches and right sides together; stitch all round. Trim and clip around curves of inset seam allowance and then press upwards. Attach back side insets to back bodice, right sides together, matching notches and fitting seamlines together carefully around extreme curves to avoid any pleats forming. Stitch, clip inset seam allowances, trim to within 7mm and press towards sideseams, then set aside.

▶3　To make up pockets, fold each one in half along foldline marked on the pattern and set against front side insets. Baste into position, raw edges matching, and set each front side inset against front bodice piece, matching notches and with right sides together. Stitch as for back side insets, trimming away inset seam allowance to within 7cm, and clipping around extreme curves to ease, as before. Press seam allowances towards sideseams. Now attach front to back bodices at side seam, and at shoulder line, easing back shoulder to match up notches. Stitch, clip

curves and press seam allowances open. Set aside.

▶4　Run a line of basting down inner stitch line of front facings as marked on your pattern, 4cm in from raw outer edge of each rever. With right sides together, place front trim against front facing, (see Fig. 1), easing around curves, and stitch. Clip curves, press towards centre front raw edge and then baste to edge, running your stitching line within 1cm of raw edge. Check raw edges match so that trim lies flat against facing. Repeat for other side, then repeat complete operation for top collar.

▶5　To make up collar, set top collar against undercollar, right sides together, and easing undercollar around curves. Stitch along long outer edge and connecting short sides to points, marked A on pattern. To set collar, open out collar so that right sides of topcollar and undercollar are uppermost, then edgestitch along long edge of undercollar, through seam allowances, close to first line of stitching, beginning and ending about 5cm each side of collar points. Trim undercollar seam allowance, clip curves, turn to right side and press. To set roll of collar, hold top collar uppermost over your hand, rolling it over as it would lie around the neck; pin along inner raw edge to set. You may find a differential of up to 1cm to be trimmed off undercollar, depending on the thickness of your fabric. Baste along pinned seamline up to points marked A at each side, then trim away excess on undercollar.

▶6　Set collar against neckline, undercollar to right side of bodice and matching notches; stitch between points B, all around neckline. Clip into points B on jacket bodice only, then continue stitching line on each side of collar along to points A. Strengthen points B with an extra line of stitching around each point and set aside.

▶7　Join front facings to back neck facing at shoulder seams, finishing 1cm before outside edge of back neck facing. Stitch and press seam allowances open. Set facings against neckline and down each front opening, right sides together and matching notches, to finish 1cm inside inner raw edge of the hemline of each front. Stitch all round, clipping into points B as before and following first line of stitching around neckline. Trim facings to 5mm, clip curves, trim corners and turn to right side. Opening out back facing and collar so that both are right side uppermost, edgestitch along neck facing through all seam allowances, machining from points B to B. Edgestitch again from front waist point, along centre front bodice opening and through seam allowances, to within 3cm of each rever point. Press carefully.

▶8   Begin to make up sleeves by marking all round contrast cuff stitchline marked on your pattern, either with pins or a line of basting. Attach contrast exactly as front facings: match notches for back sleeve, stitch, clip into curve and press towards cuff edge. Baste raw edges at cuff together, laying contrast flat against opened sleeve; make up as one. Fold each sleeve in half lengthways, right sides together, and stitch down seamline. Press seam allowances open.

▶9   To set in sleeves, start by running a line of gathering around sleevehead between notches marking attachment to seamlines on bodice. Set each sleeve into armhole openings, right sides together, matching notches and easing carefully around sleevehead. Pin, then stitch all round. Do make sure shoulder seam notch matches that on shoulder seam of bodice: the hang of the sleeve will depend on the accuracy of its angle when set into the bodice; it must be correctly positioned. Trim seam allowances, clipping curves all around armhole. Press seam allowances outwards, holding iron away from sleevehead, and applying steam only to create a smooth curved sleevehead. Next cut two pieces of domette, 15cm by 10cm, and fold each one in half lengthways so that one long edge hangs 3cm below other long edge (Fig. 1, Coat). Align folded edge of domette with raw sleevehead seam allowance so that deeper side is against sleeve, then slipstitch folded edge very loosely to shoulder seam allowance. Repeat for second piece.

▶10   Set shoulder pads against shoulder edge, aligning long thick edge of shoulder pad with armhole seamline. Slipstitch into position at top and bottom, where pad covers shoulderline (Fig. 1, Coat). To finish cuffs, turn edge to wrong side along foldline as marked on your pattern and press. Blindstitch loosely around raw cuff edge to join to sleeve.

▶11   To make up lining, begin by making pleats at centre back bodice and shoulderline, and at front side panel bust point, as marked on your pattern. Then join back to side back panels, and side back panels to front side panels, right sides together. Stitch and press seam allowances open, clipping where necessary. Make up sleeve as before, right sides together, stitching down underarm seamline and pressing seam allowances open. Set into lower half of armhole opening, matching notches and right sides together, leaving 1.5cm seam allowances at back shoulder and 1cm seam allowance free at front bodice point. Clip curves. To set in lining, attach

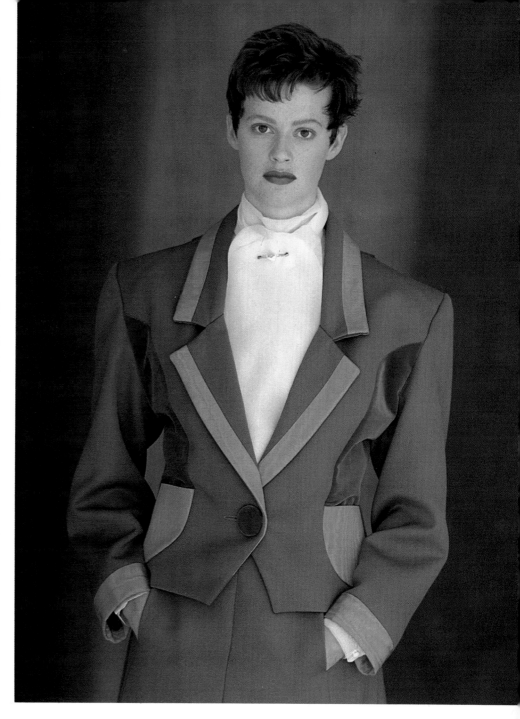

right sides of back neck lining and back neck facing, matching centre back notch, and stitch from shoulderline to shoulderline, leaving 1.5cm free at each end. Attach right sides of shoulder seams from back neck facing edge to shoulder, thus continuing first line of stitching to each shoulder edge. Lay front facing seam allowance at shoulderline towards the back, then continue to pin all round remaining sleevehead, attaching it to facing armhole, right sides together; continue down front of facing edge to hemline, matching raw edges and notches, and stitching to 10cm above hemline edge on each side. Finish by tucking sleeve linings into sleeve; repeat for other sleeve.

▶12   To finish off hem of lining, turn edge under by 5mm to wrong side and stitch all round.

Make a second turning of 1cm to wrong side and stitch round inner folded edge of lining. Press, tuck sleeve linings into sleeve, and turning jacket to wrong side, turn under 1cm at bottom of lining to wrong side, matching it to raw edge of cuff facing. Slipstitch all round, then repeat for other sleeve. You will find a fold forms naturally, giving ease of movement inside jacket. Baste underside of shoulderline to shoulder pad very loosely, matching seamlines, then attach underarm points of lining to jacket, at each side, with loose handstitches. Fold down remaining lining edges at bottom of facing and slipstitch down each side to finish.

▶13   Make buttonhole and attach button as indicated on your pattern. Press completed jacket very carefully.

Fine & Dandy
C O A T

YOU WILL NEED

3.50m of 150cm wide fabric (main)
1.40m of 120cm wide fabric (contrast 1 – velvet)
3.50m of 150cm wide lining fabric
1.40m of 50cm wide interfacing
10cm domette
1 large velvet-covered button
2 smaller velvet-covered buttons

An elegant, fully lined coat that reflects the same lines as those of the jacket. Its collar however, is 'highwayman' in style rather than tailored, and there is also a little buttoned half belt – a much favoured detail.

▶1 Attach interfacing to top collar, back neck insert, pockets and front facing pieces.

▶2 Make up exactly as Jacket instructions.

▶3 Make up exactly as Jacket instructions, but omitting pocket.

▶4 Make up as Jacket instructions (Step 5).

▶5 Make up as Jacket instructions (Step 6).

▶6 Make up exactly as Jacket instructions (Step 7). Repeat edgestitching operation at centre front openings, down to 10cm above hemline on each side, and press carefully.

▶7 Make up as Jacket instructions (Step 8).

▶8 Make up as Jacket instructions (Step 9). (See Fig.1.)

▶9 Make up half back belt by placing self and contrast belt pieces right sides together; stitch all round, allowing a gap at one long side through which to turn to right side. Trim corners, turn

fig.1

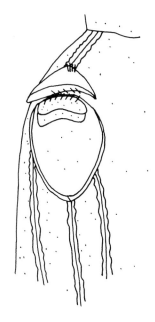

and press. Close opening with slipstitches, then place against coat centre back as marked on your pattern. Pin in position. Attach buttons, one at each side as marked, and stitch through to wrong side of coat to secure belt in place, contrast side of belt uppermost.

▶10 To make up pockets, set each pocket right sides together against lining pieces; stitch all round, leaving a gap at top straight edge through which to turn to right side. Trim corners, clip curves and turn. Press both pockets carefully. Set each pocket into position as marked on your pattern and slipstitch carefully all round curved edges to secure in place.

▶11 Make up exactly as Jacket instruction (Step 10).

▶12 Make up exactly as Jacket instructions (Step 11).

▶13 Make up exactly as Jacket instructions (Step 12). On inside of coat, attach the seam allowances of inner edges of facing at curves with loose handstitches, matching seam allowance of coat; lay it flat on ironing board or a table so as to be sure to set it accurately, and work down from waist to 25cm below waist on each side. Then starting 20cm above hemline on inside of coat and coat lining, attach lining seamline at sideseam to corresponding seamline of coat; use either very loose handstitches, or a handmade chain stitch.

▶14 Make up exactly as Jacket instructions (Step 13).

Fine & Dandy
WAISTCOAT

YOU WILL NEED

65cm of 150cm wide fabric (main)
65cm of 115cm wide fabric (contrast 2 – moiré)
65cm of 150cm wide lining fabric
1 smaller velvet-covered button

This neat little lined waistcoat has a softly gathered back cut in a contrast fabric; it is also caught in with a back belt, and fastened at the front with a single button. It follows the same design lines as those of the other clothes in this section – particularly the jacket, coat and skirt.

▶1 Join centre front panels to side front panels, right sides together and matching notches; stitch. Press seam allowances open and clip curves where necessary.

▶2 Make up back belt by folding in half lengthways, right sides together, and stitching along raw edges to make a tube. Turn, press, and with seamline facing downwards, set across back waistcoat as notched, aligning raw edges at

sideseams. Staystitch each side. Press carefully.

▶3   Join front to back waistcoat at sideseams, right sides together and matching notches, sandwiching belt inbetween. Stitch from top to bottom on each side and press seam allowances open, clipping into seamline where necessary. Join right sides together across shoulder lines, stitch, then press seam allowances open.

▶4   Make up lining, following Steps 1 and 3 as given above, then set right sides against waistcoat, matching seamlines, and working around neckline and down each front opening to hem. Stitch, then turning so that right sides of lining and waistcoat are uppermost, edgestitch along lining and through seam allowances all around neck and front opening, beginning 5cm up from front waist point, and finishing at same point on other side. Turn waistcoat back to wrong side, clip seam at curves and trim corners. Then continue stitching line along hem, leaving a gap through which to turn. Turn waistcoat to right side and slipstitch hem gap to close. Press all round. To finish armholes, fold and pin each armhole seam allowance of 1cm under to wrong side, then pin together matching seamlines. Slipstitch carefully all round, and press. Repeat for other side.

▶5   Make buttonhole and attach button as marked on your pattern.

Fine & Dandy
S K I R T

A high-waisted skirt which is both easy to make and to wear. It has a centre back zip closing, distinctive pocket interest, and is cut to flare more at the back than at the front, thus giving a really flattering line when on the move. Only one contrast fabric is used in this instance.

▶1   To make up back, join two centre back pieces, right sides together and matching notches; stitch from zip notch to hem. Baste from zip notch to top and neaten seam allowances separately, pressing them open. Attach zip to centre back opening either by machine or hand, using stabstitch, beginning at top of zip, 1cm down from top raw edge of centre back.

▶2   Attach side back pieces to centre back panels, right sides together, and matching notches; stitch from top to bottom. Neaten seam allowances separately and press open.

YOU WILL NEED

1.90m of 150cm wide fabric (main)
55cm of 115cm wide fabric (contrast 2 – moiré)
15cm of 150cm wide lining fabric
1 skirt zip, 20cm long
2 skirt loops

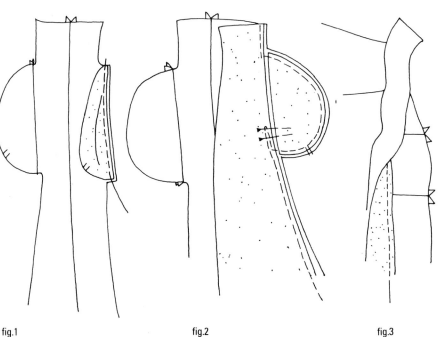

fig.1   fig.2   fig.3

▶3 Attach centre front pieces, right sides together and matching notches; stitch from top to bottom. Neaten seam allowances separately and press open. Attach one pocket bag lining to each extended 'ear' piece on centre front skirt panels, right sides together and with notches on curve at lower sides; stitch from top to bottom, 1cm in from raw edges. Press lining outwards on each side. (See Fig.1.)

▶4 Attach self pocket bags to front side panels, matching notches and raw edges of side seams. Stitch from top to bottom, trim pocket bag seam allowances and press outwards. Now lay front side panels with attached bags over centre front panels, right sides together and aligning pocket 'ear' and seam allowance edges; stitch from top to bottom, around pocket bags. Stitch 6cm up each seamline from bottom of pocket (as shown Fig. 2), keeping all seam allowances clear and facing towards sides.

▶5 Join front to back at side seams, right sides together; stitch from top to bottom. Neaten seam allowances separately and press open. Make up facing exactly as skirt, placing facing pieces right sides together and stitching from top to bottom. Press seam allowances open, then neaten inner edge of facing all round.

▶6 Mark all around waist of skirt with a line of basting, starting 4.5cm down from top raw edge as marked on your pattern. Then working from centre front point, attach shortest curve of waist contrast fabric, right sides together, along marked line (see Fig.3). Stitch all round, clip curves of contrast and, folding up towards top of skirt, press flat all round. Pin into position flat along top raw edge of skirt, then place facing against contrast, right sides together and matching seamlines. Stitch all round, trim facing seam allowances, then edgestitch around facing only, through seam allowances, beginning and ending 3cm from centre back. Clip seam allowances and press to wrong side.

▶7 To encase top of zip, set facing to wrong side of skirt as pressed. Trimming corners carefully, fold in zip seam allowances to wrong side, then slipstitch down length of facing and close to zip edge on each side. Press. Slipstitch down each facing seam allowance, to lower end of facing, catching to skirt seam allowances only all the way round. Attach hook and eye to top of centre back zip opening, and adjust hem length as necessary. Allowing 1.5cm turning allowance, neaten raw edge of hem and turn up to wrong side. Then stitching close to inner neatened edge of hem, stitch around hemline, through to right side. On wrong side, lay each pocket flat against centre front seam allowance and baste loosely to hold in place. Attach hanging loops to side seam facing allowances. Press skirt.

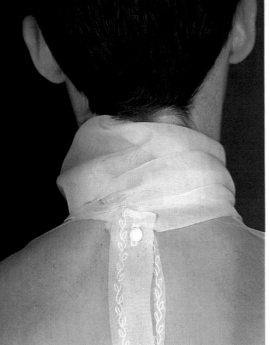

Fine & Dandy
B L O U S E

A neat tailored blouse with centre back buttoning and a double rolled collar which lengthens to form a stock when wrapped and tied at the front. There is embroidery interest on the front bodice, which is carried through onto the centre back opening and repeated on the cuffs. The front bodice is finely pleated to complete this strongly feminine look.

YOU WILL NEED
2m of 120cm wide fabric
7 tiny buttons

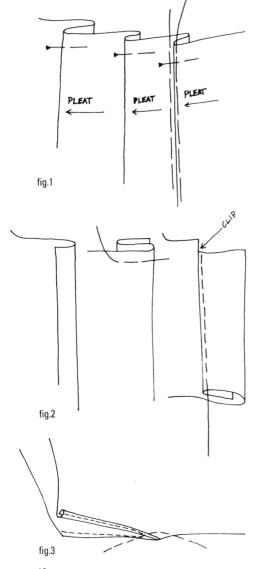

fig.1

fig.2

fig.3

▶1   Make pleats, tucking vertically down each side of front bodice as shown on your pattern; to form each pleat as shown in Fig. 1, use straight basting lines as a guide to match up tucking lines. Press. Stitch through centre of each pleat either with a straight stitch or with any combination of the embroidery stitches available on your machine. (The blouse in the photograph features leaves, stars and waves stitched in an outward direction on each side of the front bodice.) Press again carefully.

▶2   Make centre back opening by folding 3cm to right side down back opening, following top and bottom fold notch marks. Press, then fold 3cm back again, as notched, to wrong side; stitch across top of self facing to neaten. Fold back again to right side, press, baste fold in place, and then either run a line of straight stitching from neck to hem, 1cm in from inner folded edge, or use a chosen embroidery stitch from your machine – in this instance, leaves. (See Fig.2.)

▶3   Join front bodice and two back bodice pieces at shoulder line, with wrong sides together, for French seams. (Remember that for working French seams, you must think in terms of making up the shirt entirely on the right side, forming a tuck in those seams to pull them to the inside - it helps to remember to join the shirt pieces *wrong sides facing*, rather than in the normal way.) Stitch 5mm in from edge across shoulders, press, turn to other side, and stitch across shoulders again, 5mm in from edge and enclosing raw edges. Press French seams towards back. Join sideseams by same method. Press and set aside.

▶4   To make up sleeves, begin by turning 5mm under to wrong side at bottom of split for cuff opening, then stitch up to point so that the turning allowance narrows away to nothing at the top. Turn under another 5mm to wrong side and repeat stitching. Press. Fold sleeve in half lengthways, right sides together, so that the top of the split comes at the foldline, stitch across the top of each split to secure weak spot as shown in Fig.3. Press. Make up sleeves by stitching a French seam as before, at underarm seamlines: wrong sides together, then right sides together. Press seam allowances towards cuff splits.

▶5   Set left sleeve into left armhole, wrong sides together, matching notches and underarm seamlines; stitch all round. Turn blouse to wrong side, finish off French seam as before, and then press French seam towards cuff. Repeat operation for right sleeve.

▶6   To attach cuffs, press 3cm of self facing, as notched and shown on your pattern, to wrong side. Then attach the other long raw edge of cuff to raw edge of sleeve, right sides together and overlapping split by 1cm on each side. Stitch all round. Fold back facing and undercuff, right side against top cuff, and stitch across each short end. Turn back cuff to right side, tuck in raw seam allowances, and slipstitch all round inside of cuff, attaching it to original stitching line. Press. Add embroidery, if required, close to where cuff joins sleeve and stitching through cuff seam allowances; remember to thread ends of cotton through to inside with a needle to finish neatly and unobtrusively. Repeat for the other cuff.

▶7   Attach necktie to neck opening, beginning at centre front notch and working round each side to points on back facing. Stitch all round, beginning and ending at inner edge of back facing, and then clip into seam allowance at joining point to ease. Fold necktie back on itself, right sides together and matching centre front notches and then, starting at inner facing edge, stitch along to each end, pivot needle and continue stitching line to finish across short end of tie. Repeat for other side. Trim corners of ties and turn to right side. Fold remaining raw neck edge of neck tie to inside and pin around as you did for cuffs; slipstitch inside of neck to close. Press inner neck edge of facing and then secure with a few handstitches to strengthen.

▶8   Make buttonholes and attach buttons as marked on the pattern to centre back opening and cuffs, wrapping cuff so that buttonhole is on front side of cuff, away from underarm seamline. Press.

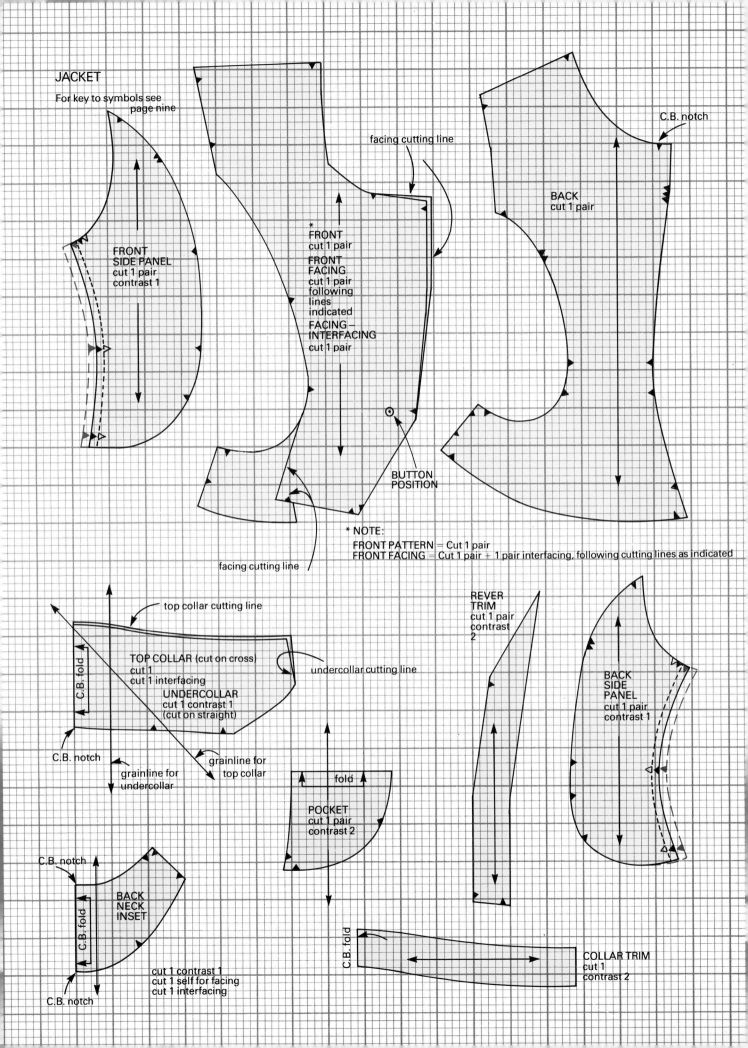

JACKET

For key to symbols see
page nine

FRONT
SIDE PANEL
cut 1 pair
contrast 1

facing cutting line

*
FRONT
cut 1 pair
FRONT
FACING
cut 1 pair
following
lines
indicated
FACING –
INTERFACING
cut 1 pair

BUTTON
POSITION

facing cutting line

BACK
cut 1 pair

C.B. notch

* NOTE:
FRONT PATTERN = Cut 1 pair
FRONT FACING = Cut 1 pair + 1 pair interfacing, following cutting lines as indicated

top collar cutting line

TOP COLLAR (cut on cross)
cut 1
cut 1 interfacing
UNDERCOLLAR
cut 1 contrast 1
(cut on straight)

undercollar cutting line

C.B. fold

C.B. notch

grainline for
undercollar

grainline for
top collar

fold

POCKET
cut 1 pair
contrast 2

REVER
TRIM
cut 1 pair
contrast
2

BACK
SIDE
PANEL
cut 1 pair
contrast 1

C.B. notch

C.B. fold

BACK
NECK
INSET

cut 1 contrast 1
cut 1 self for facing
cut 1 interfacing

C.B. notch

C.B. fold

COLLAR TRIM
cut 1
contrast 2

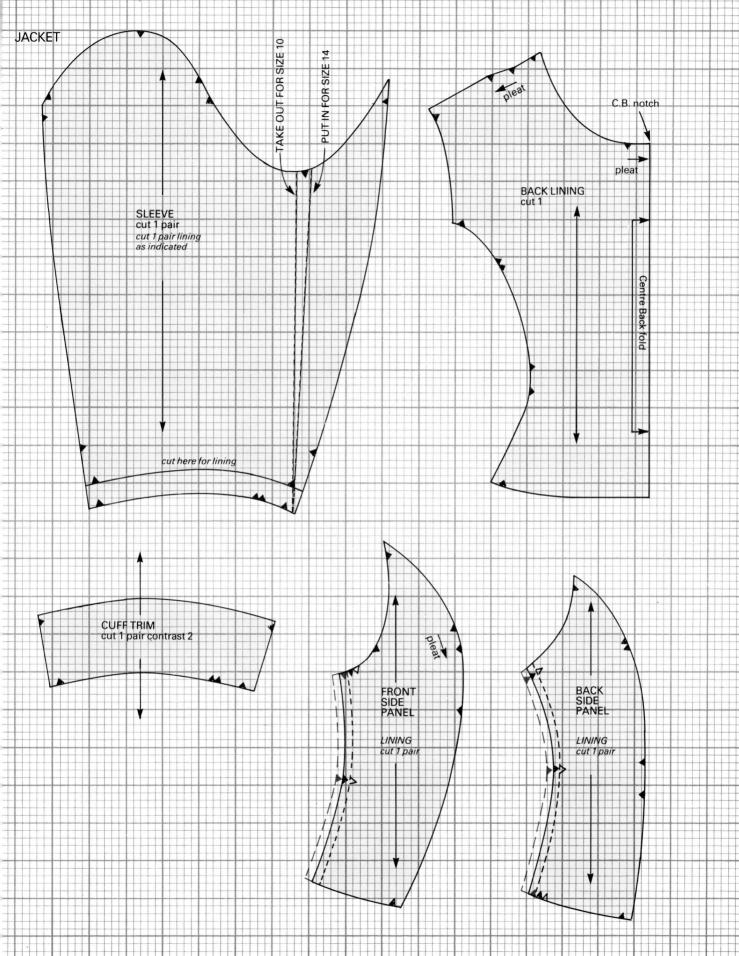

JACKET

SLEEVE
cut 1 pair
*cut 1 pair lining
as indicated*

TAKE OUT FOR SIZE 10

PUT IN FOR SIZE 14

cut here for lining

BACK LINING
cut 1

pleat

C.B. notch

pleat

Centre Back fold

CUFF TRIM
cut 1 pair contrast 2

FRONT
SIDE
PANEL

*LINING
cut 1 pair*

pleat

BACK
SIDE
PANEL

*LINING
cut 1 pair*

21

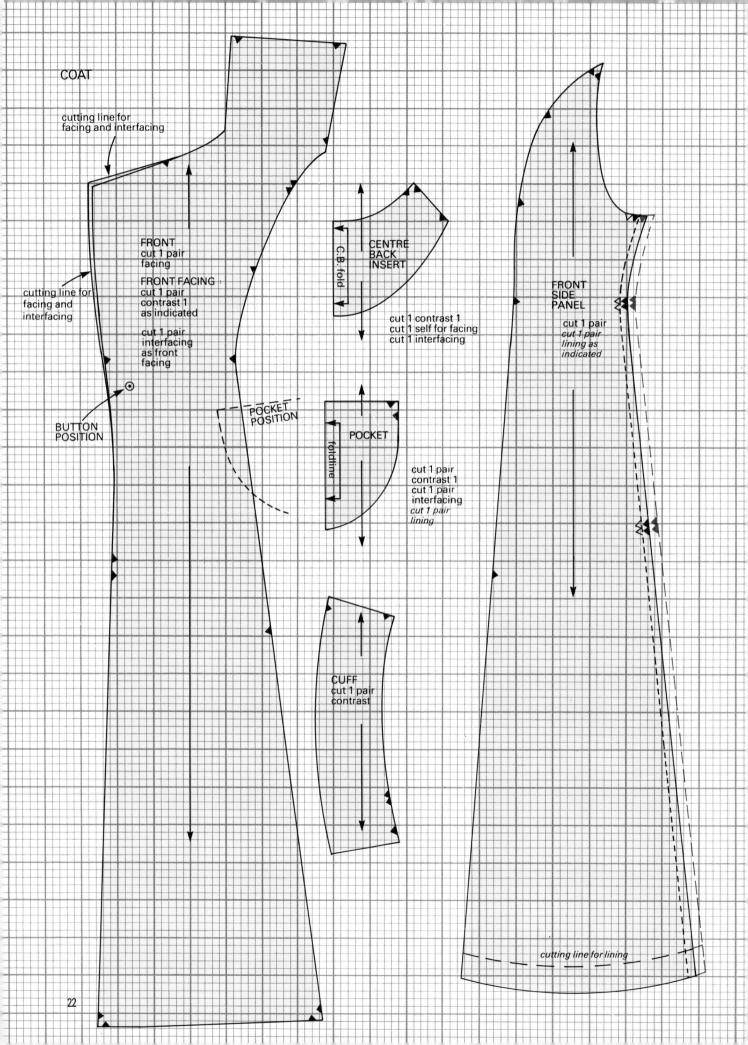

COAT

cutting line for
facing and interfacing

cutting line for
facing and
interfacing

FRONT
cut 1 pair
facing

FRONT FACING
cut 1 pair
contrast 1
as indicated

cut 1 pair
interfacing
as front
facing

BUTTON
POSITION

POCKET
POSITION

C.B. fold

CENTRE
BACK
INSERT

cut 1 contrast 1
cut 1 self for facing
cut 1 interfacing

FRONT
SIDE
PANEL

cut 1 pair
cut 1 pair
lining as
indicated

foldline

POCKET

cut 1 pair
contrast 1
cut 1 pair
interfacing
cut 1 pair
lining

CUFF
cut 1 pair
contrast

cutting line for lining

22

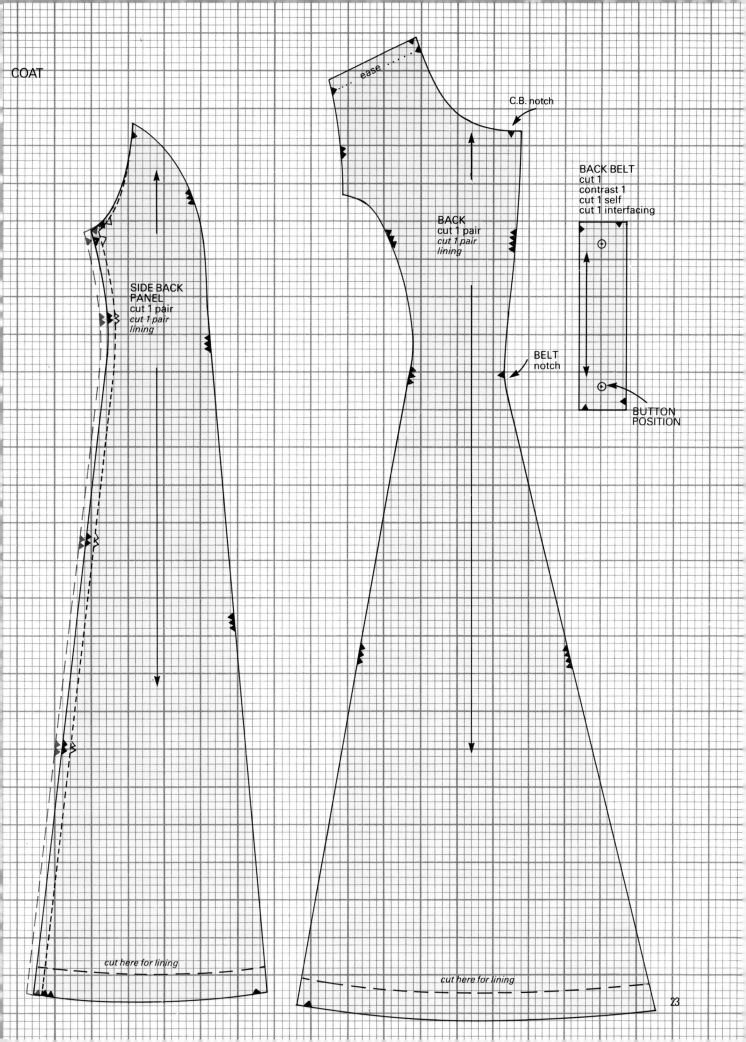

COAT

SIDE BACK
PANEL
cut 1 pair
*cut 1 pair
lining*

ease

C.B. notch

BACK
cut 1 pair
*cut 1 pair
lining*

BELT
notch

BACK BELT
cut 1
contrast 1
cut 1 self
cut 1 interfacing

BUTTON
POSITION

cut here for lining

cut here for lining

23

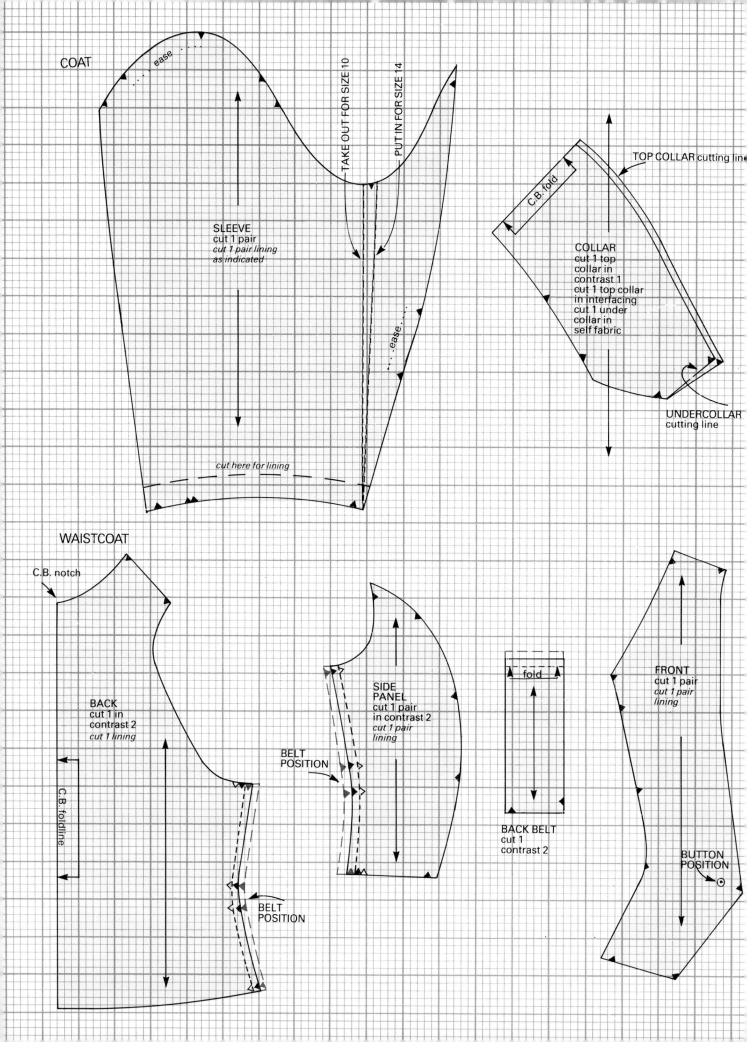

COAT

ease

TAKE OUT FOR SIZE 10

PUT IN FOR SIZE 14

SLEEVE
cut 1 pair
*cut 1 pair lining
as indicated*

ease

cut here for lining

TOP COLLAR cutting line

C.B. fold

COLLAR
cut 1 top
collar in
contrast 1
cut 1 top collar
in interfacing
cut 1 under
collar in
self fabric

UNDERCOLLAR
cutting line

WAISTCOAT

C.B. notch

BACK
cut 1 in
contrast 2
cut 1 lining

C.B. foldline

BELT
POSITION

BELT
POSITION

SIDE
PANEL
cut 1 pair
in contrast 2
*cut 1 pair
lining*

fold

BACK BELT
cut 1
contrast 2

FRONT
cut 1 pair
*cut 1 pair
lining*

BUTTON
POSITION

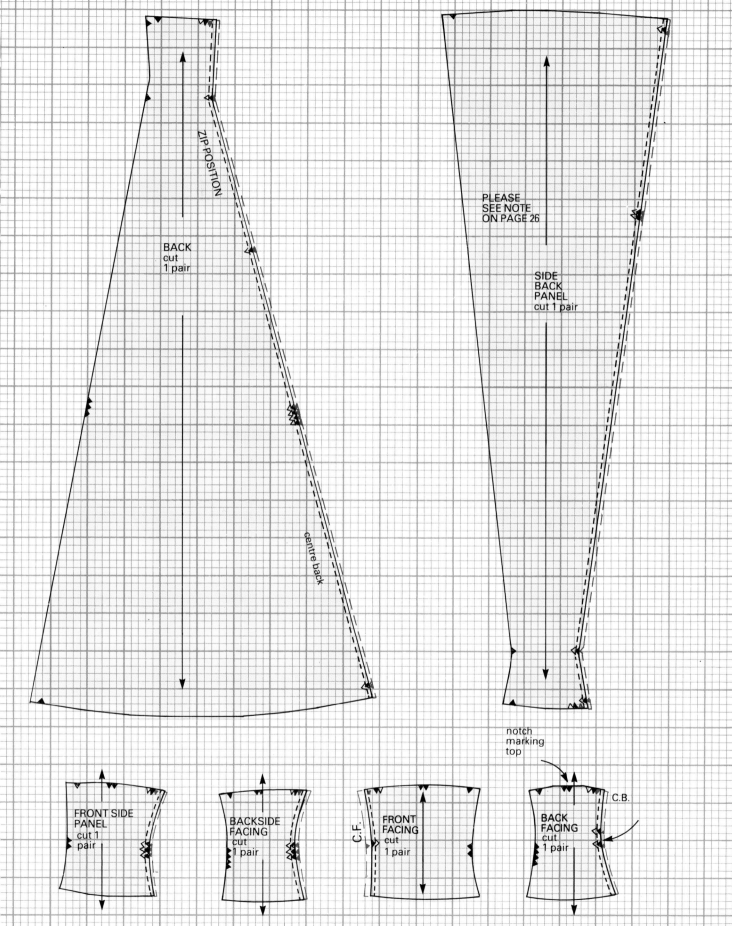

SKIRT

ZIP POSITION

BACK
cut
1 pair

centre back

PLEASE
SEE NOTE
ON PAGE 26

SIDE
BACK
PANEL
cut 1 pair

notch
marking
top

C.B.

FRONT SIDE
PANEL
cut 1
pair

BACKSIDE
FACING
cut
1 pair

C.F.

FRONT
FACING
cut
1 pair

BACK
FACING
cut
1 pair

25

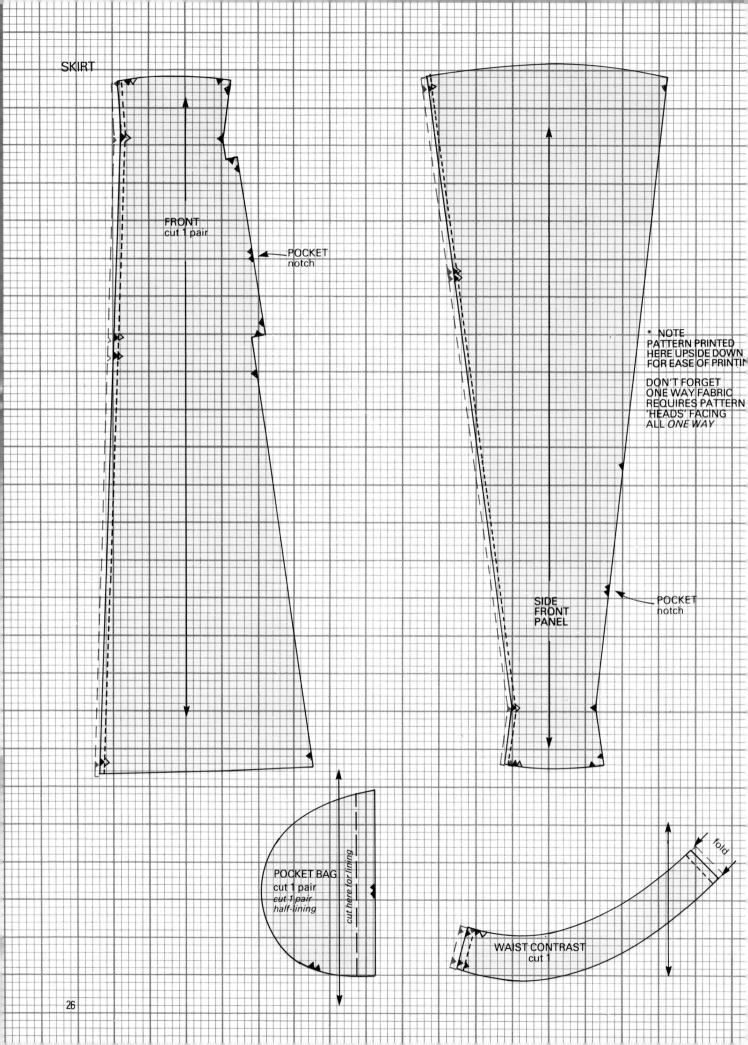

SKIRT

FRONT
cut 1 pair

POCKET
notch

SIDE
FRONT
PANEL

POCKET
notch

* NOTE
PATTERN PRINTED
HERE UPSIDE DOWN
FOR EASE OF PRINTIN

DON'T FORGET
ONE WAY FABRIC
REQUIRES PATTERN
'HEADS' FACING
ALL *ONE WAY*

POCKET BAG
cut 1 pair
*cut 1 pair
half-lining*

cut here for lining

WAIST CONTRAST
cut 1

fold

26

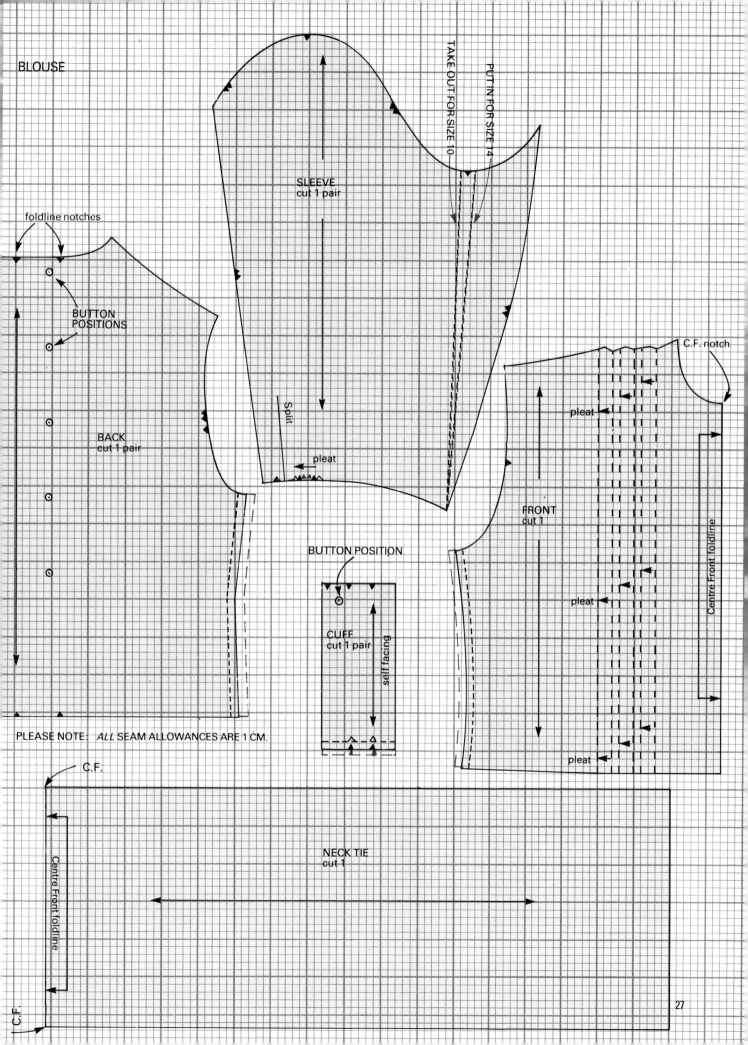

BLOUSE

SLEEVE
cut 1 pair

TAKE OUT FOR SIZE 10

PUT IN FOR SIZE 14

foldline notches

BUTTON
POSITIONS

BACK
cut 1 pair

Split

pleat

C.F. notch

pleat

FRONT
cut 1

pleat

Centre Front foldline

BUTTON POSITION

CUFF
cut 1 pair

self facing

pleat

PLEASE NOTE: *ALL* SEAM ALLOWANCES ARE 1 CM.

C.F.

NECK TIE
cut 1

Centre Front foldline

C.F.

27

Having looked far and wide for a really warm pure wool jersey which could be worn unlined and yet would still retain its shape, the jersey shown here proved perfect. The result is a sophisticated sports-orientated outfit which owes something to my experience in designing wetsuits and diving suits for professionals and enthusiastic amateurs alike. The flashes of colour on shoulders and legs seemed a good way of 'lifting' the jersey, whilst at the same time echoing the idea of using strip-like side panels on each garment. The funnel neckline and loose, comfortable cut of the arms are practical yet still interesting; the fabric and knit balaclava-style hood will ensure head and ears stay warm throughout the worst weather conditions. (For notes on sewing jersey, refer to page 8.)

Sports Chic

The rib-knit pieces, the pattern pieces for which are given on pages 38–43, can be knitted by hand or machine. Four-ply wool was used, working to a tension of 13 stitches per 2.5cm (counting horizontally along a row) and 11 rows per 2.5cm (counting vertically). Knit up a 10cm sample square before starting work to check your tension, adjusting the needle size or tension as necessary for a smaller or larger stitch. Count the stitches and rows per 2.5cm, and referring to the sizes of the pattern pieces, multiply accordingly for the number of stitches to cast on and the number of rows to work for the correct size of each piece. If in doubt, knit lengths to roughly the size required and then trim to the correct shape, neatening the edges to prevent unravelling. Each piece can then be stitched into place and any excess trimmed off afterwards.

Sports Chic S K I R T

YOU WILL NEED

80cm of 170cm wide fabric
6×50g balls of 4-ply wool (for 2 knitted strips)
1.55cm of 170cm wide lining
curved petersham
1 zip, 20cm long
2 pairs hooks and eyes

The waist of this simply cut, but fully lined, skirt is set against a curved backing for ease and comfort, with a centre back zip fastening. Design detail is strongly represented in the knitted side panels.

▶1 Join back skirt pieces at centre back, right sides together, and stitch from notch marking bottom of zip to hem. Baste from zip notch to waist, then press seam allowances open. Set zip behind basted opening, with top of zip 1cm down from raw edge of opening; stabstitch into place by hand. Press, then remove basting.

▶2 Set knitted side strips against sides of back skirt, right sides together. Working from hem edge upwards, pin and then stitch from hem to waist on each side. (If your knitted strip is longer than the back skirt edge, overlap at the waist rather than the hem, since the waistline will be double-stitched. It is thus less likely to fray if any excess needs to be cut off than if placed at hemline.) Join front skirt to knitted side strips, right sides together, and stitch from hem to waist as before. Press all seam allowances open.

▶3 Make up lining exactly as for skirt, omitting zip insertion. Press all seam allowances open and then, with wrong sides together, set lining inside skirt, matching centre back and side strip seamlines. Pin all around waistline; baste.

▶4 Attach waistline backing exactly as for Pants, Steps 5 and 7, inserting a skirt loop at the centre of each knitted side strip at waistline. At centre back zip, slipstitch lining to its backing, all the way round. Stitch again across knitted side strip seam allowance at waistline to strengthen.

▶5 To finish hem, turn up 3cm at raw hem edge to wrong side, pin, and then stitch 1cm in from raw edge, through to right side, from knitted side strip edge to knitted side strip edge, on back and front skirt. Slipstitch remaining knitted hem edges to secure. To finish hem lining, turn up 5mm to wrong side and stitch all round. Turn up 1cm again to wrong side and edgestitch close to inner folded edge of hem, machining all the way round and through to the right side.

Sports Chic
T O P

The top shown here carries the same knit and side panel features of all the other garments in this outfit, while a curved neckline strip, ending in a buttoned tab front, completes the look. Wear it with the pants or skirt, adding the coat for warmth.

▶1　Attach knitted shoulder strips to front and back bodice pieces, right sides together and matching notches. On each side, stitch from neck to cuff edge and press seam allowances away from knitted strips. Trim knitted strips at cuff edge if necessary, neatening each strip by hand to prevent unravelling.

▶2　Attach underarm side strip to each side of back bodice and sleeve, right sides together and maching notches. Stitch all round from hem to cuff on each side. Join side strips to front bodice pieces, right sides together and matching notches, then stitch all round from hem to cuff on each side, as for back. Press all seam allowances open.

▶3　Join centre front seamline, right sides together; stitch from top to bottom. Press seam allowances open. Fold neckband in half lengthways, matching notches but with wrong sides together. Baste along long raw edges to set. Now attach neckband to neck opening, right sides together and matching notches, setting front of neckband into front bodice at front seamline so that lower front edge of neckband overlaps the raw edge of bodice by 2cm. (See Fig.1.) Stitch all round from 1cm below raw edge of centre front bodice to same point at other side. At base of centre front bodice opening, clip very carefully into seamline at each corner, then tuck each 'tail' of neckband inside bodice front, right band over left band. Turn inside, as shown in Fig.2, so that inside of front bodice is uppermost and 'tails' are set behind front opening seam allowance at centre front base; pin across to secure. Check line of setting on right side is horizontal, then on wrong side stitch across tab ends of neckband to secure. Stitch again 5mm down from first line of stitching. Trim tab seam allowance, layering it so that it lies flat behind bodice, then press all seam allowances away from neck edge, round neck opening. Press tab flat.

▶4　Finish cuffs and hemline exactly as for Coat, Steps 6 and 7.

▶5　Make buttonholes and attach buttons as shown on your pattern.

YOU WILL NEED

1.50cm of 170cm wide fabric
6×50g balls of 4-ply wool (for 2 knitted strips)
3 buttons

fig.1

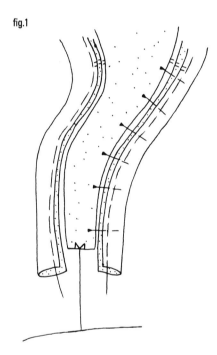

fig.2

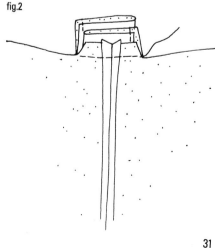

Sports Chic JACKET

Featuring single-breasted front buttoning, this jacket also has important shoulder and armline detail in the form of knitted strips that follow through to knitted cuffs. Side panels echo the line of each strip, and there is a funnel-shaped neckline for further interest. A simple belt, attached to a prongless buckle, completes the effect, casual yet sophisticated. The jacket can be worn with the skirt or pants, or over the top or dress.

▶1 Trim knitted strips to pattern shape if not already knitted to shape, neatening raw edges by staystitching or overlocking carefully to avoid stretching or unravelling.

▶2 Join shoulder knitted strip pieces to back jacket, right sides together; stitch from neck cuff edge, since it can later be trimmed. Join remaining long edge of each knitted strip to front jacket pieces, right sides together; stitch from neck to cuff down each side. Press all seam allowances away from knitted strips.

▶3 Follow instructions exactly as for Coat, Step 2.

▶4 Attach side strips to back jacket, right sides together and matching notches; stitch from cuff to hem on each side. Now attach strips to front jacket pieces, right sides together and matching notches; stitch from cuff to hem. Press seam allowances open.

▶5 Finish cuffs exactly as for Pants, Step 6, being sure to place cuff seamline to join of back jacket and side strip, on each side.

▶6 To finish hemline of jacket, follow instructions for Coat, Steps 7 and 8.

▶7 Make shoulder pads and attach to jacket in exactly the same way as described for Coat, Step 9.

▶8 To make up belt, fold in half lengthways, right sides together, and stitch around one short side and one long side. Trim corner, turn and press. To attach prongless buckle to raw edge of belt, thread 4cm of belt through the wrong side, fold under raw edge and stitch across by hand to set in place.

▶9 To finish, begin by measuring your waistpoint, add 2-3cm for blousing, and then make belt loops in side seams by hand.

YOU WILL NEED
1.55cm of 170cm wide fabric
8×50g balls of 4-ply wool (for 2 knitted strips and 2 cuffs)
1 pair shoulder pads (curved)
30cm lining (to cover pads)
1 buckle (prongless)
5 buttons

Sports Chic BALACLAVA

Easy to slip on and off over the head, this jersey and knit fabric hood is really quick and easy to make. It is long enough to keep the neck well covered, as well as the head and ears, and will keep you really warm.

▶1 Join long edges of knitted strip to each side of balaclava head, right sides together and matching notches, so that it reaches from face to neck edge. Stitch down each side from top to bottom and press seam allowances away from knitted strip.

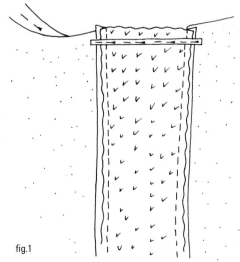

fig.1

YOU WILL NEED
50cm of 170cm wide fabric
2×50g balls 4-ply wood (for 1 knitted strip)
15cm of 5mm wide tape

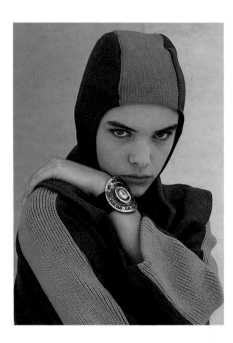

▶2 Join centre front seamline, right sides together, and stitch from top to bottom. Press seam allowances open.

▶3 With inside of knitted strip uppermost, attach a piece of tape across the short face end of the knitted strip so that the inner edge of the strip is level with the 1.5cm seamline. Stitch tape to knitted strip through centre, making sure you do not stretch the knitting: it should measure 9cm from seamline to seamline. (See Fig.1.)

▶4 Turn back 1.5cm at face edge of hood to inside and pin all round. On wrong side of turnback, stitch from edge of knitted strip around and under chin to finish at other edge of knitted strip; stitch 1cm in from folded face edge, through to right side. Slipstitch along remaining knitted foldback to finish.

▶5 To finish hem, repeat Step 4, but omitting tape. Press.

Sports Chic
P A N T S

YOU WILL NEED
1m of 170cm wide fabric
10×50g balls of 4-ply wool (for 2 knitted strips and 2 cuffs)
30cm of 5mm wide tape
curved petersham
1 zip, 20cm long
2 pairs hooks and eyes

The lines of the pants shown here follow those of the skirt, with waistline backing and a zip inserted centre back. Knitted strips run in an arc from high on each hip down the length of the leg; the hems are knitted cuffs.

▶1 Join back to front side seams at hip by placing right sides together and stitching from waist to top of knitted side strip on each side. Press seam allowances open.

▶2 Run a line of staystitching around curved top of knitted inserts, slightly inside the cutting line; trim knitted side strips to pattern shape if they have not already been knitted to shape, remembering to neaten below cutting line before cutting to shape. Set each side strip against side seams at hip point and pin all round from front to back pants, working from cuff edge upwards on each side. Stitch, press seam allowances away from strip on each side; catch curved seam allowances of side strips to hip seam allowances, with a few handstitches.

▶3 Fold each leg in half lengthways so that right sides of inside leg seamline come together; stitch from crutch to hem. Press seam allowances open.

▶4 Turn one leg right side to outside and set it inside other leg so that right sides of crutchline meet. Pin all round, matching notches and undercrutch point, then stitch from centre front waistline to centre back notch marking bottom of zip. Baste from zip point to waistline at back. To strengthen seamline, pin tape into position over first stitching line, beginning above crutch point at centre front notch and finishing at centre back zip notch. Stitch through centre of tape. Press seam allowances open and set zip behind basting and centre back, beginning 1cm down from raw waistline edge. Pin, then stab-stitch by hand to set in place. Press; remove basting.

▶5 To finish waistline, baste around upper edge, then cut curved waistline backing to fit, allowing an overlap of 2cm at each end. Set into position flat against right side of pants, so that backing overlaps raw waistline edge by 1cm, and wider, outer curved edge of backing faces away from waistline. Pin into position, easing all round waistline, tucking in 2cm at each end to wrong side. Then edgestitch all around narrower curved edge of backing, through to wrong side. (See Fig.1.)

▶6 To prepare knitted ankle cuffs, first stitch short ends together by hand with a length of wool so that a cylinder is formed. If made on a double-bed machine, fold in half so that seam allowances are on the wrong side, inside finished cuff; if made on a single bed, stitch flat to wrong

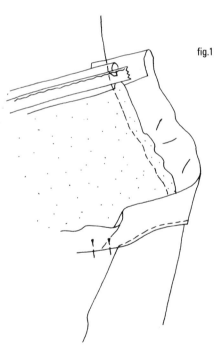

fig.1

side. Next run a line of gathering stitches around the bottom of each cuff, gather slightly and then attach a cuff to each leg, right sides together and matching inside leg seamlines, before stitching all round.

▶7   Turn waistline backing to inside of pants and press; catch with a few handstitches against seam allowances at centre back, centre front and side seams. Attach a hook and eye to the inside of folded back waistline backing to finish.

Sports Chic
C O A T

YOU WILL NEED

2.80cm of 170cm wide fabric

6×50 balls of 4-ply wool (for 2 knitted strips)

50cm of 5mm wide tape

1 pair shoulder pads (curved)

30cm lining (to cover pads)

5 buttons

(Note: cut back on fold of fabric, then open out fabric to cut front pieces separately, fitting smaller pattern pieces into remaining fabric)

A front buttoning, double-breasted unlined coat. The strong design detail is in the sections of knitted fabric inserted across the shoulder and along the arm; this effect is repeated in the side panels. There are inset pockets at the hipline and a funnel neckline for added warmth.

▶1 Run a line of basting stitches, from top to bottom, down each coat front foldline. Trim knitted shoulder strips (as for Pants, Step 2) if not already knitted to shape, then attach a shoulder strip to each shoulderline of back coat, right sides together and working from the cuff edge up to neckline. Stitch from cuff to neckline, then set remaining edge of each strip against front coat pieces, right sides together; stitch from cuff to neck on each side. Press seam allowances away from knitted strips on front and back coat.

▶2 Attach back neck facing to shoulder facing strips, right sides together and matching notches; stitch. Press seam allowances towards strip on each shoulder, then attach front edge of each shoulder strip to front self facings, right sides together and matching notches; stitch across each side. Press seam allowances towards facing strips as described before.

▶3 Fold right side of neck facing back onto right side of coat, matching seamlines and centre front notches; pin, then stitch all round. Now run a line of tape all around neckline, beginning at front fold edge and placing tape so that left edge is in line with first line of stitching. Stitch tape into position as indicated in Fig.1. Trim seam allowance points and turn so that right sides of facing and coat are uppermost. Edgestitch round neck edge of facing; to set facing to inside, machine from front edge of one facing strip to the other. Fold facing back to inside of coat and press carefully into position.

▶4 Attach a half pocket piece to each front panel of coat, right sides together; stitch from top to bottom, then press seam allowances open. Attach a pocket bag to each side strip, right sides together, matching notches and pocket bags. Stitch from cuff to hem, following curved line of pocket bag all the way round. Stitch up seamline from bottom pocket corner to pocket opening notch, as shown in Fig.2.

▶5 Press seam allowances open, clipping into back seam allowance of pocket to allow it to lie flat. Attach side strips to back coat, right sides together and matching notches; stitch from cuff to hem on each side. Press seam allowances open.

▶6 To finish cuffs, turn up 3.5cm to inside of each sleeve and pin, easing gently around curves. Stitch 1cm away from inner raw edge of cuff from one knitted strip edge to other, then slipstitch remaining facing to wrong side of each knitted strip.

▶7 To finish hemline, fold back self facing at centre front openings, as marked on your pattern, so that right sides come together. Stitch across self facings, 3.5cm above raw edges. Turn facings back to wrong side, then pin up 3.5cm around remaining raw edge of hemline. Stitch

1cm in from inner raw folded edge of hemline, machining all the way round from front edge to front edge of coat, through to right side.

▶8   Pin self facings at centre front openings back to wrong side along foldback basting line. To set, press from top to bottom down each front coat piece. Make buttonholes and attach buttons as marked on your pattern.

▶9   For shoulder pads, cover a pair of pads as described in Summer Breeze, Duster Coat, Step 9. Set in position on shoulderline so that they just overlap your shoulder edge; their centre lines should lie exactly along the centre of each knitted strip. Stitch loosely into position by hand, basting along each knitted strip seamline. Next wrap neck facings back into position over the top of each pad, stitching again by hand along each seamline to hold firmly in place. This will ensure that the knitted strips will not be pulled out of shape across shoulderlines.

fig.1

fig.2

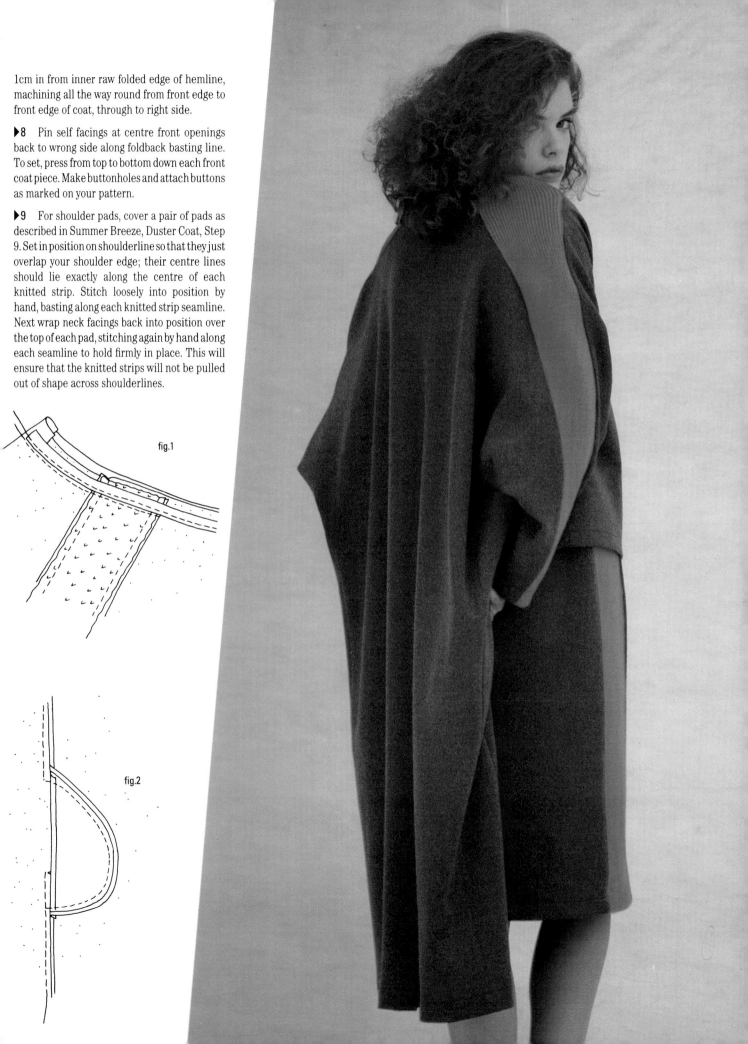

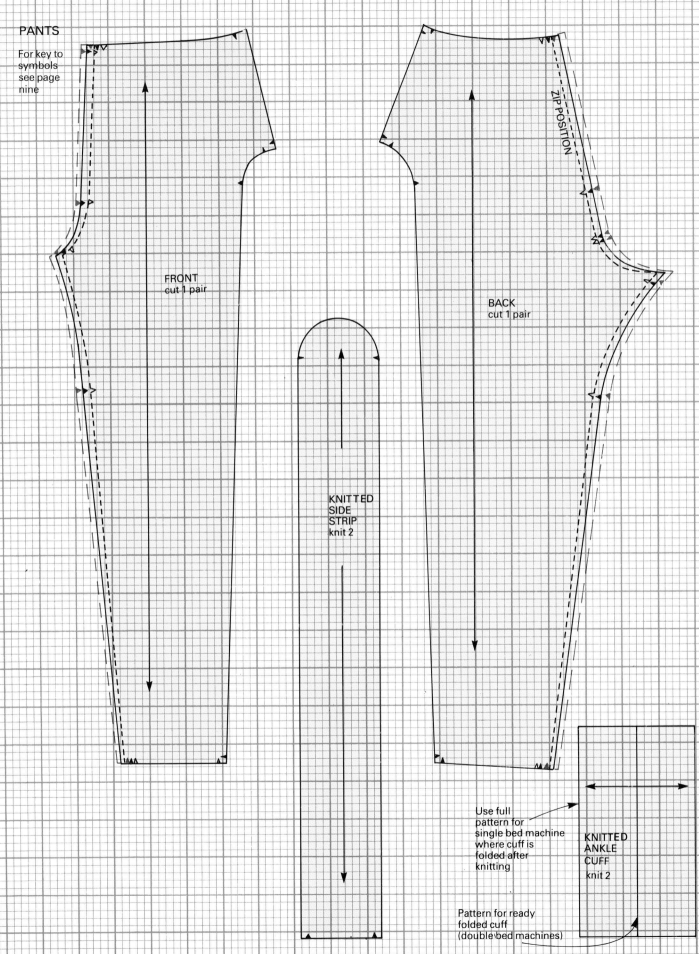

PANTS

For key to
symbols
see page
nine

FRONT
cut 1 pair

BACK
cut 1 pair

ZIP POSITION

KNITTED
SIDE
STRIP
knit 2

Use full
pattern for
single bed machine
where cuff is
folded after
knitting

KNITTED
ANKLE
CUFF
knit 2

Pattern for ready
folded cuff
(double bed machines)

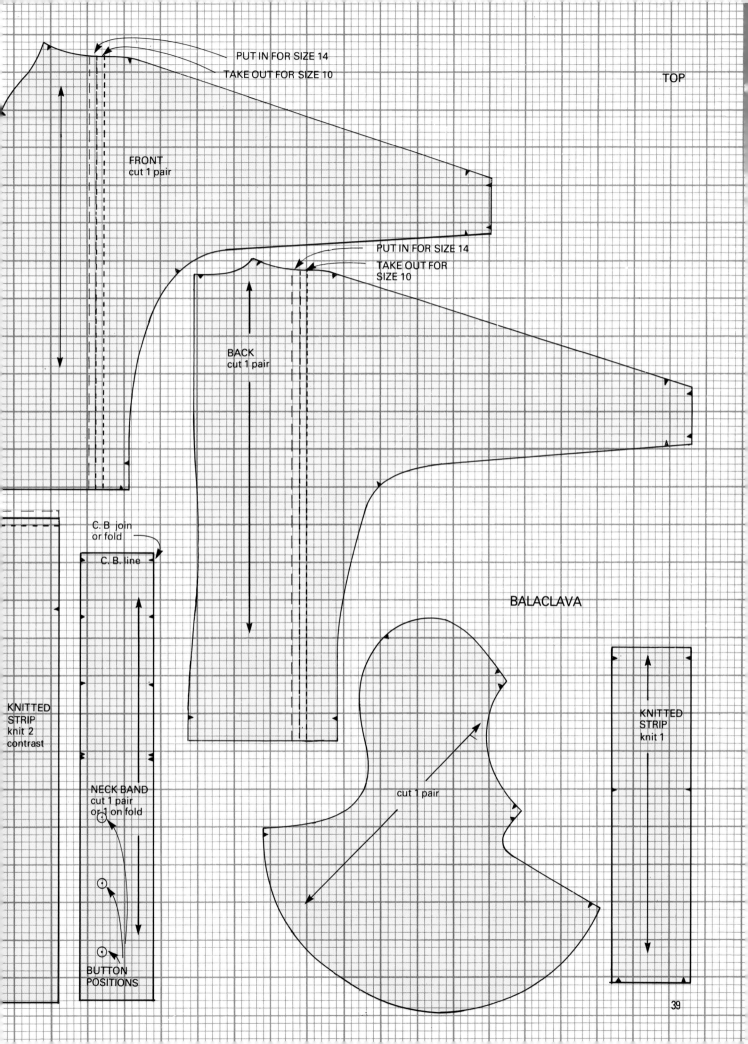

PUT IN FOR SIZE 14
TAKE OUT FOR SIZE 10

TOP

FRONT
cut 1 pair

PUT IN FOR SIZE 14
TAKE OUT FOR
SIZE 10

BACK
cut 1 pair

C. B. join
or fold

C. B. line

BALACLAVA

KNITTED
STRIP
knit 2
contrast

KNITTED
STRIP
knit 1

cut 1 pair

NECK BAND
cut 1 pair
or 1 on fold

BUTTON
POSITIONS

39

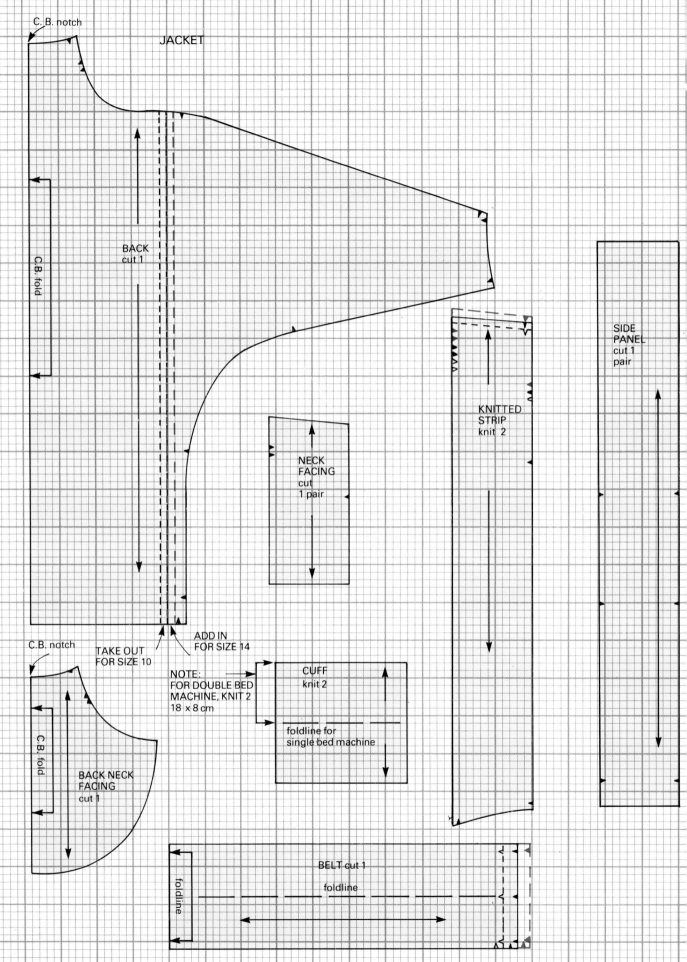

C.B. notch

JACKET

C.B. fold

BACK
cut 1

SIDE
PANEL
cut 1
pair

KNITTED
STRIP
knit 2

NECK
FACING
cut
1 pair

TAKE OUT
FOR SIZE 10

ADD IN
FOR SIZE 14

C.B. notch

C.B. fold

BACK NECK
FACING
cut 1

NOTE:
FOR DOUBLE BED
MACHINE, KNIT 2
18 x 8 cm

CUFF
knit 2

foldline for
single bed machine

foldline

BELT cut 1

foldline

40

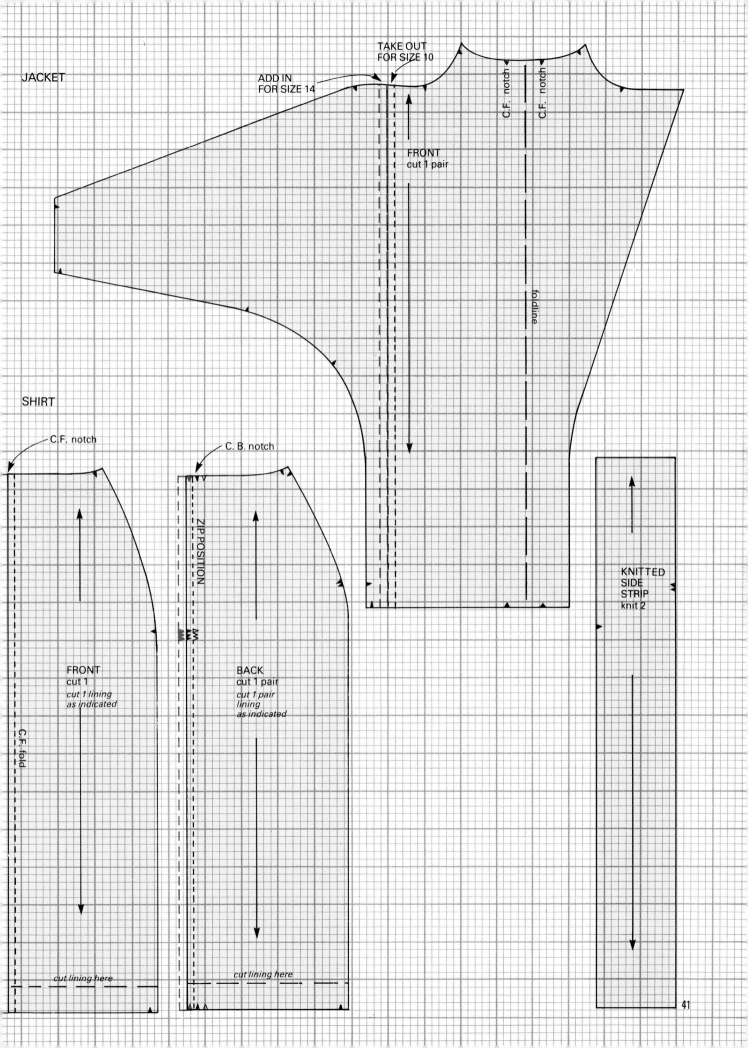

JACKET

ADD IN
FOR SIZE 14

TAKE OUT
FOR SIZE 10

C.F. notch

C.F. notch

FRONT
cut 1 pair

foldline

SHIRT

C.F. notch

C. B. notch

ZIP POSITION

FRONT
cut 1
*cut 1 lining
as indicated*

C.F. fold

BACK
cut 1 pair
*cut 1 pair
lining
as indicated*

KNITTED
SIDE
STRIP
knit 2

cut lining here

cut lining here

41

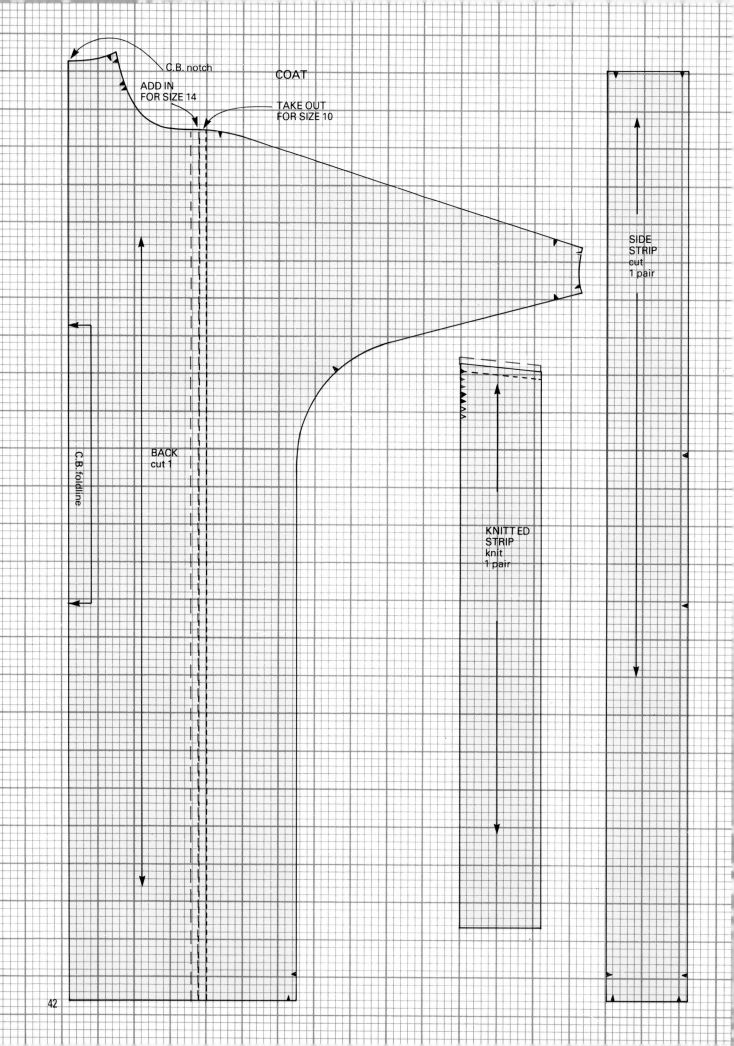

C.B. notch

ADD IN
FOR SIZE 14

COAT

TAKE OUT
FOR SIZE 10

SIDE
STRIP
cut
1 pair

C.B. foldline

BACK
cut 1

KNITTED
STRIP
knit
1 pair

42

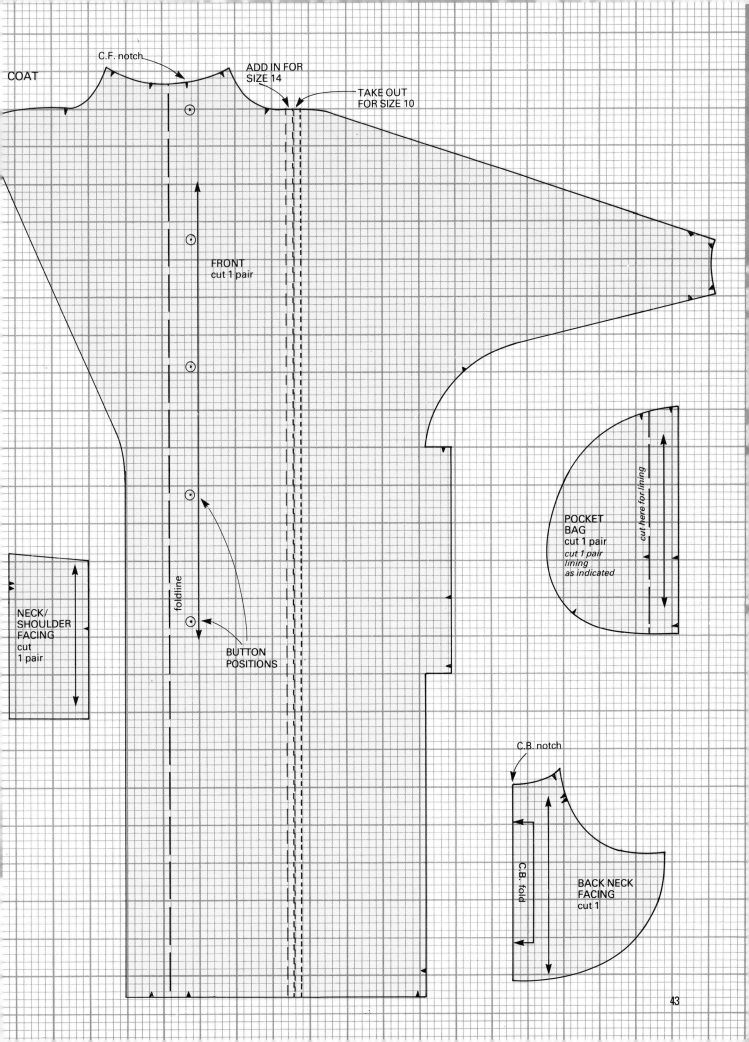

COAT

C.F. notch

ADD IN FOR
SIZE 14

TAKE OUT
FOR SIZE 10

FRONT
cut 1 pair

foldline

BUTTON
POSITIONS

NECK/
SHOULDER
FACING
cut
1 pair

POCKET
BAG
cut 1 pair
cut 1 pair
lining
as indicated

cut here for lining

C.B. notch

C.B. fold

BACK NECK
FACING
cut 1

The brief for this outfit was that the clothes should be stylish enough to wear to town, yet practical enough for wearing layers underneath to keep warm, so that long walks and cold weather could be taken in their stride. The coat is in a thick warm wool, its capacious collar in a soft fake fur. The half belt at the back gives a slightly twenties feel, Poiret being a designer much turned to for inspiration. Following the lines of the coat, the suit is also half-belted on both the back of the jacket and skirt. The revers and cuffs offer much potential for using a contrast fabric, a design feature which could be repeated in the panelling on the sides and under the sleeves if the material was suitable. The skirt follows the same narrow straight line, but flares out below the knee; the co-ordinating shirt and tracksuit-style pants are sportier still in effect.

Country House

Country House
J A C K E T

YOU WILL NEED

1.60m of 150cm wide fabric
1.20m of 150cm wide contrast fabric
1.50m of 150cm wide lining fabric
(or 1.70m of 1.15m wide fabric)
1m interfacing
1 pair of curved shoulder pads
5 covered buttons

fig.1

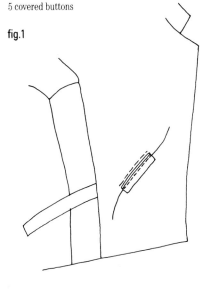

fig.2

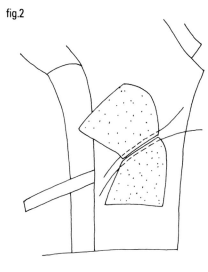

fig.3

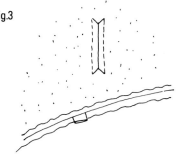

The raglan sleeved jacket shown is fully lined, has contrast revers, pocket welts and half belt, and sports covered buttons. It is equally suitable for town as well as country wear, and the inset side panels could be made up in a bright contrast colour to offset a dark base fabric. Mix textures of the same colour tones for a more sophisticated finish.

▶1   Attach interfacings to front and back facings, top collar, cuffs, back belt pieces and pocket welts.

▶2   Join front and back sleeve at shoulderline, matching notches. Stitch, press seam allowances open and repeat for other sleeve. Join sleeve inset to front and back sleeve, stitch, and press seam allowances open; repeat for other sleeve. Set aside.

▶3   To make up back belt, fold each in half lengthways, right sides together, and stitch down long side and one short end only. Trim, turn to right side and press. Set each belt piece in position as marked against front bodice, facing them towards the back and matching seam allowances, with belt seamlines facing downwards. Staystitch into position.

▶4   To make up pockets, firstly fold pocket welts in half lengthways, with right sides together, and stitch across both short ends. Trim, turn to right side, and baste along remaining long raw edges. Press carefully. Set in position on front jacket pieces as shown in Fig. 1, aligning raw edge of welt to cutting line of each pocket. Stitch across welt from end to end. Now place underpocket bag on top of welt, matching raw edges and overlapping evenly each side. Set top pocket bag in the same way (see Fig.2) and stitch across as marked, 1cm away from raw edges, beginning and ending at welt edges. Cut along each front jacket piece as marked to open up pockets, finishing 1cm inside each welt edge, then cut into corners of each line of stitching as shown in Fig.3. Lay jacket flat with right sides uppermost, turn pockets to inside and pin welts and pocket bags into position so that each pocket bag edge matches on the wrong side,

trimming away if necessary. Stitch, or sew by hand, around each pocket bag, catching in the small 'V' shape at the corner of each pocket split, formed when each pocket opening was cut. Press flat carefully, and on outside of jacket, slipstitch ends of each welt firmly in place.

▶5   Join bodice insets to front and back bodice pieces, matching notches and encasing belt at each side. Stitch and press seam allowances open. Attach left sleeve to left bodice around raglan line, matching notches and underarm seamlines. Stitch, then press seam allowances open. Repeat for right sleeve. Trim seam allowances where necessary, staystitch around neckline from point B to B as marked on pattern, and set aside.

▶6   To make up collar, attach top collar to undercollar, right sides together, and stitch around outer curved edge and each side to points marked A. Trim points and seam allowances where necessary. Turning so that right sides of top and undercollar are uppermost, edgestitch all along undercollar through seam allowances, beginning and ending stitching at each side of collar points. Turn top collar to outside, press, then staystitch remaining raw edges of collar together to hold, making sure to align raw edges carefully to allow for the 'roll' of the collar.

▶7   Attach undercollar to right side of bodice neckline, matching notches and points A. Stitch all round, pivoting needle and clipping into points B on bodice to ease. Trim corners and undercollar seam allowance and clip into neckline around curves. With facing and top collar facing upwards, and with the bodice lying to the right of the collar, edgestitch along facing from 5cm to front of each shoulder seam and through seam allowances, and all around the back of neck.

▶8   Attach front and back neck facings at shoulder seams, stitch and press open. Attach facings to jacket, right sides together, matching seamlines and encasing collar. Stitch from bottom of left front opening, up and around neckline, pivoting needle at point B to finish as you began, at the bottom of right front opening of jacket. Trim corners and turn so that right sides of facing and bodice of jacket are uppermost. Edgestitch up bodice opening through seam allowances, beginning at top button point and breaking off stitching 5cm before rever

point and then starting again 5cm beyond the rever point to finish at point A. Repeat for other side and press carefully.

▶9   Make up cuffs by folding each top cuff in half so that right sides of underarm seamline come together. Stitch across and repeat for undercuffs, trimming seam allowances of undercuffs only. Set undercuff inside top cuff, right sides together, and stitch around narrower opening. Trim, then turn both top and undercollar cuff uppermost, edgestitching around undercuff, through seam allowances. Press and repeat for other cuff. Now attach each top cuff to a sleeve, matching notches and stitch all round. Trim and pin top and under-cuff together roughly halfway up to hold in posi-tion. On inside of cuff, slipstitch undercuff flat against top cuff, sewing along top cuff seam allowance.

▶10   Make up lining following the same routine as for the jacket. Make pleat in centre back neck and hem of lining, stitching down about 3cm from the top, and basting the bottom pleat, which may later have to be adjusted. Press pleat into position from top to bottom. Press remaining seam allowances open, as before. To set in lining, pin into position on inside of jacket,

right sides together, beginning at centre back neck point. Matching shoulder seams, work around each side to finish 10cm above raw hem edge. Stitch. Set one shoulder pad in each shoulder, attaching by hand with a few loose stitches, then tuck a sleeve lining into each sleeve. Match raw edges of undercuff and sleeve lining at cuff edge, and slipstitch all round. You will find a pleat forms to allow for ease. Baste lining loosely to jacket across shoulderline and at underarm points.

▶11   To finish hem, fold front facing back onto jacket front at hemline, right sides together, and stitch across facing. Trim facing seam allowance and turn to right side. Fold up hem to wrong side as marked and baste into position close to fold. Blindstitch hem and press. Catch-stitch raw lower edges of facings where they lie across hem, fold down lower edge of lining and then, with raw edges of hem and hem lining aligned, slipstitch along length of hem. Slip-stitch remainder of lining to facing each side (you will find a pleat forms naturally at the lower edge of the facing).

▶12   Make buttonholes and attach buttons as marked on your pattern, at front opening and on back belt.

Country House
S K I R T

Featuring the same side-panel detail as the jacket, this elegantly cut straight skirt flares out just below the knee in a very flattering manner and allows for ease of movement. It is also buttoned at the centre back point with a half belt.

▶1   Make darts in side panels and press open. Set inverted box pleat on lower back skirt as shown on pattern and staystitch across top seam allowance to hold in place. Join to back skirt, right sides together, and stitch. Trim one seam allowance, press both upwards and on right side, edgestitch along back skirt through all seam allowances.

▶2   Attach interfacing to back belt pieces, then fold each piece in half lengthways and stitch around one short edge and along long edge only. Trim, turn and press each belt piece. Set into position on back skirt, laying each belt directly over the top of seamline joining back skirt to

lower back skirt, seam allowance edges aligned. Pin in place.

▶3   Join side panels to front skirt, right sides together and matching notches. Stitch and then press seam allowances open. Repeat for back skirt, tacking 20cm down from waistline at right back seam only, ready for zip insertion, and enclosing raw seam allowances of belt on each side. Press seam allowances open and on inside of skirt; stitch each belt seam allowance to each side panel seam allowance to flatten. Attach other side of seam allowance loosely by hand, across back of skirt, above pleat.

▶4   Attach zip by hand or machine, laying directly under basted seamline and just below waistline. Stitch all round, close to teeth of zip, using a longer understitch and a very short stabstitch on top if you work by hand. Remove basting and press.

▶5   Make up lining exactly as skirt, omitting belt inserts and leaving right back seam allow-ance open for zip as before. Set lining inside skirt, wrong sides together; then matching front and back, and seamlines, pin and staystitch all

round. Turn under seam allowance at zip opening, pin, then sew by hand all the way round zip opening to secure. Turn skirt inside out so that wrong sides of lining and skirt are uppermost at lower zip point, then baste loosely to secure together.

▶6   Attach waistband to waist of skirt, right sides together and matching raw edges, and overlapping left back skirt at zip point by 3cm. Stitch all round, trim layers of seam allowance, then fold short ends in half, right sides together, and stitch across, pivoting needle at right back overlap to join stitching line to zip point. Trim points, turn to right side, then insert waistband stiffening inside waistband so that it sits against the outside of the waistband. Turn inside waistband seam allowance to wrap over and cover stiffening on the wrong side, and pin or baste so that fold of inside waistband lies just over original stitching line. Insert hanging loops at side seams, then on right side stitch all around waistline along seamline, joining skirt to waistband, through underside of waistband. Press and attach hook and bar at back opening.

▶7   To finish hemline, neaten skirt and turn up as notched on the pattern or as required. Slipstitch all around hem. Turn 5mm to wrong side at bottom edge of lining and stitch all round. Turn in 1cm again to wrong side and stitch all round close to inner folded edge of lining. Press, make buttonhole and attach covered button to back belt as marked on pattern.

Country House
S H I R T

YOU WILL NEED

1.95m of 150cm wide fabric
40cm of 150cm wide contrast fabric
40cm of interfacing
13 buttons

A loosely designed tailored shirt which is cut on the same lines as the Country House Jacket, Coat, Pants and Skirt. It has contrast collar and cuffs, a double-breasted front closing, patch pockets and an optional buttoned half belt. Make it up as illustrated, in a fine, striped man's shirting fabric with contrast collar and cuffs, or in silk crêpe-de-chine with the skirt or pants for evening dressing.

▶1 Make up sleeves by attaching front to back sleeve at shoulderline, right sides together and matching notches, and stitch. Attach under-sleeve panel to front and back sleeve, right sides together and matching notches. Stitch, leaving open at split point of back sleeve for cuff. Neaten all seam allowances and press open. Staystitch cuff pleats into position, pointing them towards the back as shown on pattern.

▶2 Make up bodice, attaching back bodice to side panels, right sides together and matching notches. Stitch, neaten seam allowances separately and press open. Repeat for front bodice pieces, leaving a gap through which to insert back belt pieces, and finish as before.

▶3 Make up back belt, folding each in half lengthways, right sides together, and stitch around one short and long side only. Trim, turn to right side, press and insert into gap left in each front sideseam. Stitch into position, raw edges matching, and neaten belt seam allowance against front bodice seam allowance.

▶4 Attach one sleeve to each armhole opening, right sides together and matching notches, and stitch all round. Neaten and press seam allowances open.

▶5 To make up collar, attach interfacing to top collar, then attach top to undercollar, right sides together, and stitch along outer curved edge and two sides. Trim corners and undercollar seam allowance; turn to right side. To set on collar, open out top collar and undercollar so that right sides are uppermost, edgestitch on undercollar through seam allowances, around long curved edge. Press. Staystitch along remaining raw edges of collar, aligning top with undercollar raw

edges. Attach collar to bodice neckline, beginning and ending at centre front point, matching undercollar to right side of bodice, and seamlines. Stitch all round; trim and layer seam allowances, clipping around curves. Neaten down front shirt facing edges, then fold each front facing back on itself, right sides together and matching centre front points (see Fig.1).

▶6 Neaten outer curved edge of back neck facing. Attach around neckline matching notches, sandwiching the collar and overlapping turned-back facing on front bodice. Stitch along original stitching line, clip curves and then open out the collar so that right sides of facing and collar are uppermost. Edgestitch around neck facing from centre front to centre front point, through all seam allowances. Roll facings to wrong side, press, then slipstitch facings to seam allowances, and neck facing to front facing as shown in Fig.2.

▶7 To make cuffs, place right sides of cuff and sleeve edge together, overlapping each pressed-back split opening by 1cm. Stitch all round and trim seam allowances. Fold cuff in half lengthways, right sides together, and stitch across each short end. Trim seam allowances and turn to right side. Turn under seam allowance along inside cuff edge and pin, just overlapping first stitching line. On right side, stitch along original seamline between sleeve and cuff, all the way round, catching inside cuff edge in stitching line. Press, then slipstitch inner pressed seam allowance of back split to wrong side of sleeve. Repeat for other cuff.

▶8 To finish hem, turn front facings back on themselves as marked on your pattern, right sides together; stitch across facings. Trim, neaten remaining raw hem edge, turn back facings to wrong side, and stitch along inner neatened edge of shirt from facing edge to facing edge. Press.

▶9 To attach pockets, neaten all round each pocket, then turn back facing edge, right sides together, and stitch across top and bottom to hold. Trim, turn to right side, and press, also pressing remaining seam allowances into position around pocket. Set in position on front bodice, matching opening edge to front side seams and edgestitch across top, down inner side, across bottom and up 6cm on outer side to finish. Press, make buttonholes and attach buttons as shown on pattern, on front bodice, cuffs and at back belt.

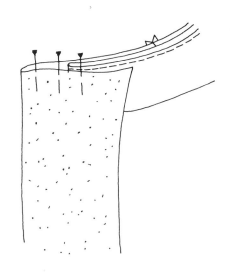

fig.1

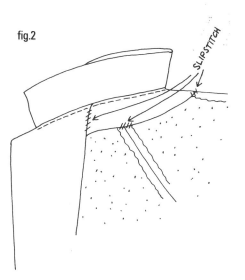

fig.2

Country House

P A N T S

YOU WILL NEED

1.40cm of 150cm wide fabric
10cm of 150cm wide contrast fabric
3cm wide waistband stiffening
1 20cm skirt zip
1 hook and bar

These simple pants with side panels are made up with single front pleats, centre back zip closing, patch pockets and contrast waistband and ankle cuffs.

▶1   Make darts in back pants and press towards side seams. Make darts in side panels and press open, splitting darts to within 2cm of points to enable each one to lie flat.

▶2   Join back to side pants, right sides together and matching notches. Stitch, neaten seam allowances separately and press open. Join front to side pants as before.

▶3   Make and attach pockets exactly as for Shirt (Step 9) and press.

▶4   Finish each leg of pants by placing right sides together at inside leg seamline and stitching from top to bottom. Neaten seam allowances separately and press open. Now attach left to right leg at crutch, matching seamlines, and

stitch downwards from centre front waist point, around crutch, to finish at centre back lower zip point. Trim, neaten seam allowances separately and press open. Baste zip opening closed.

▶5   Insert zip by hand or machine, laying directly under basted seamline and just below waistline. Stitch all round close to teeth of zip or, if sewing by hand, use a longer understitch and a very short stabstitch on top. Remove basting and press. Now attach placket to right back zip position, setting flat behind right seam allowance of zip. Stitch to seam allowance only to secure.

▶6   Make darts in front waistline as shown on pattern and staystitch. Attach waistband, right sides together, matching centre front points and overlapping at right back to enclose top of zip placket. Then proceed exactly as for Skirt. (Step 6).

▶7   Make pleats in bottom of each pants leg, facing them towards the back. Then make up cuffs, folding each cuff right sides together so that shorter ends align. Stitch across, turn to right side, and press seam allowances open. Now attach a cuff to the bottom of a pants leg, matching inner leg seamline. Stitch all round, trim and folding back half the cuff to the inside, turn under inner seam allowance so that the fold lies just over the first stitching line. On right side, stitch all around along seamlines, joining cuff to pants, and at the same time catching in inner folded edge of cuff. Repeat for remaining leg and press carefully.

Country House
C O A T

Following the same design lines as the Country House Jacket, this roomy, loosely cut and fully lined winter coat is made up in heavy wool with fake fur collar and cuffs. When using very bulky fabrics such as the fake fur featured here, you should add 5cm to the outside edge of both your collar and rever patterns, to allow the collar to roll properly. The buttoned half belt is optional, since the coat also looks marvellous when worn straight, and could easily be lengthened to mid-calf for an authentic Chicago Gangster-style look. Again, side panels enable you to use contrast textures to even greater effect.

▶1 Attach interfacings to top collar, top cuffs, front facings, back neck facing and pocket welts.

▶2–7 Make up exactly as Jacket.

▶8 Having made up exactly as Jacket, edge-stitch along front facings through seam allowances, from top buttonhole level to 10cm above hemline, on each front edge of coat.

▶9–12 Continue to make up exactly as for Jacket.

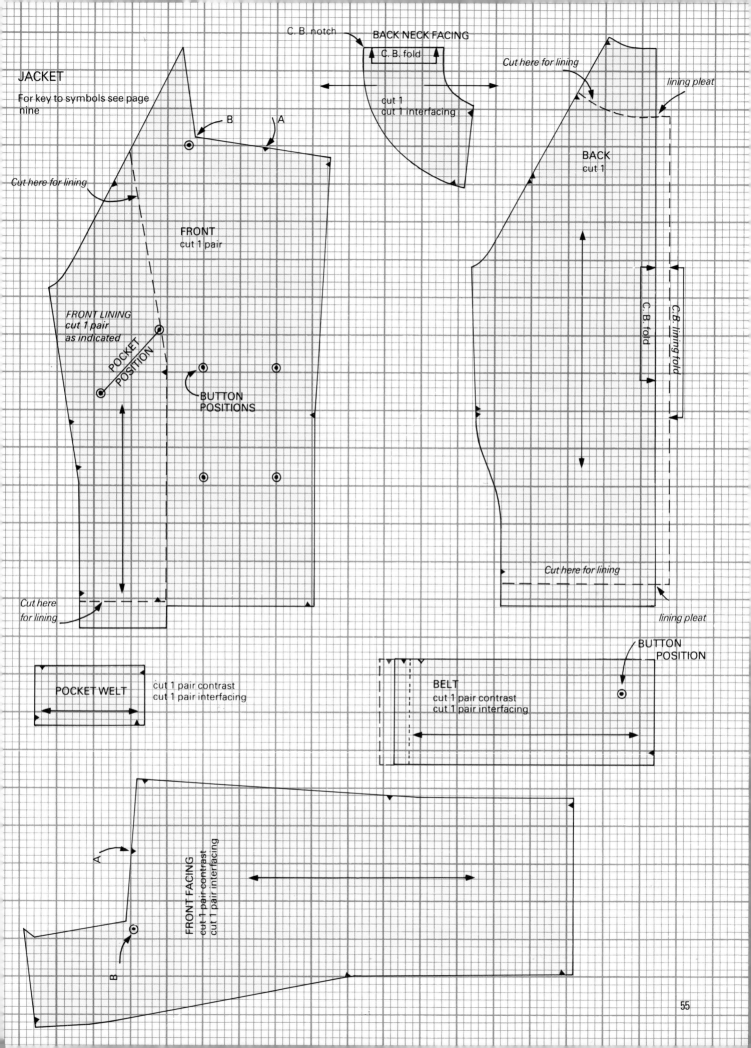

JACKET

For key to symbols see page nine

Cut here for lining

FRONT
cut 1 pair

FRONT LINING
cut 1 pair
as indicated

POCKET
POSITION

BUTTON
POSITIONS

Cut here
for lining

B   A

C. B. notch

BACK NECK FACING

C. B. fold

cut 1
cut 1 interfacing

Cut here for lining

lining pleat

BACK
cut 1

C. B. fold

C.B. lining fold

Cut here for lining

lining pleat

POCKET WELT   cut 1 pair contrast
cut 1 pair interfacing

BELT
cut 1 pair contrast
cut 1 pair interfacing

BUTTON
POSITION

FRONT FACING
cut 1 pair contrast
cut 1 pair interfacing

A

B

55

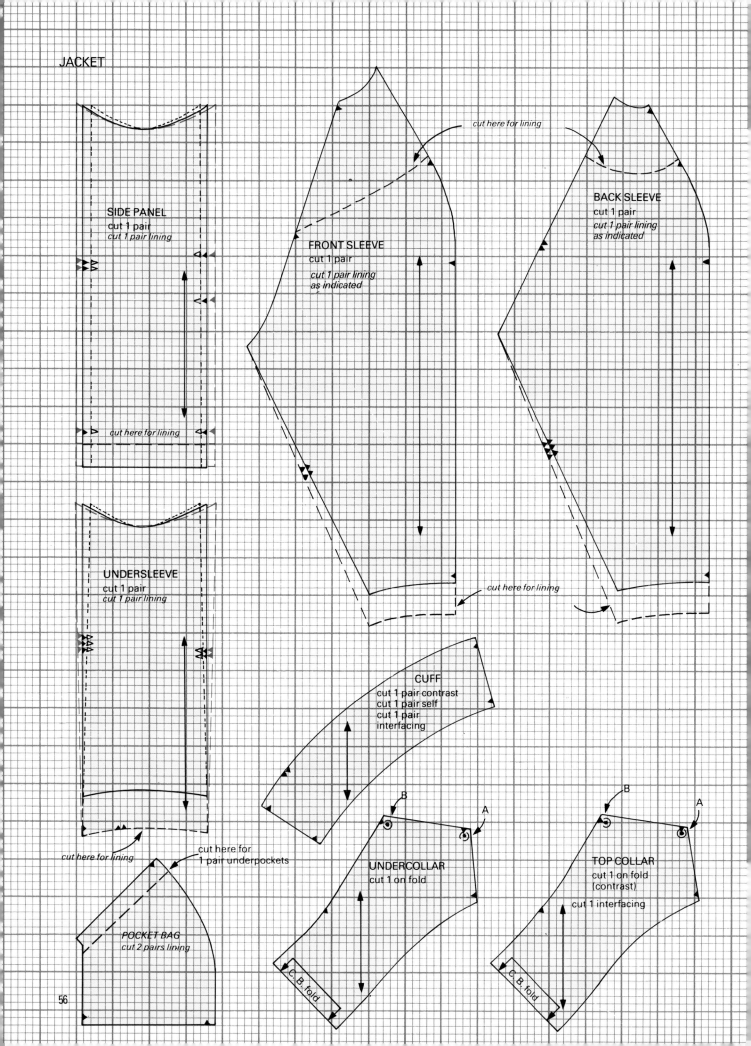

JACKET

SIDE PANEL
cut 1 pair
cut 1 pair lining

cut here for lining

UNDERSLEEVE
cut 1 pair
cut 1 pair lining

cut here for lining

FRONT SLEEVE
cut 1 pair

*cut 1 pair lining
as indicated*

cut here for lining

BACK SLEEVE
cut 1 pair

*cut 1 pair lining
as indicated*

cut here for lining

CUFF
cut 1 pair contrast
cut 1 pair self
cut 1 pair
interfacing

*cut here for
1 pair underpockets*

POCKET BAG
cut 2 pairs lining

B

A

UNDERCOLLAR
cut 1 on fold

C. B. fold

B

A

TOP COLLAR
cut 1 on fold
(contrast)

cut 1 interfacing

C. B. fold

SKIRT

FRONT
cut 1
cut 1 lining

C.F. fold

cut here for lining

DART POSITION

SIDE PANEL
cut 1 pair
cut 1 pair lining

RIGHT BACK ZIP POSITION

cut here for lining

BACK
cut 1
cut 1 lining

C.B. fold

WAISTBAND
cut 1 on fold

fold

LOWER BACK PANEL
cut 1
cut 1 lining

fold

C.B. fold

cut here for lining

BUTTON POSITION

BACK BELT
cut 1 pair contrast
cut 1 pair interfacing

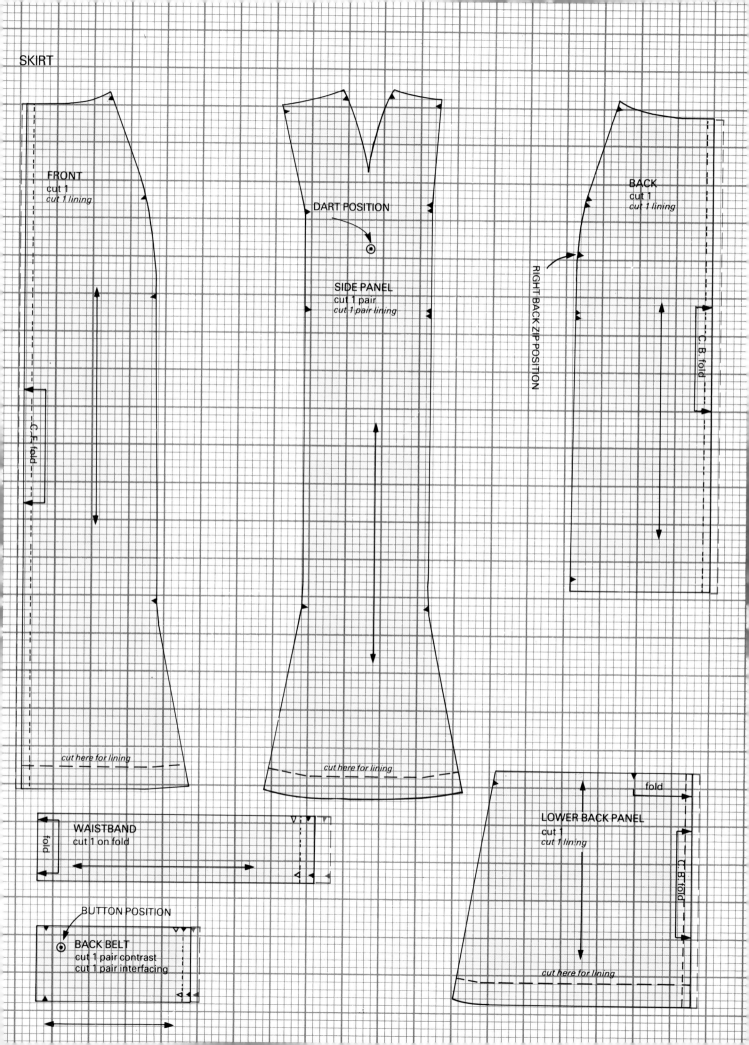

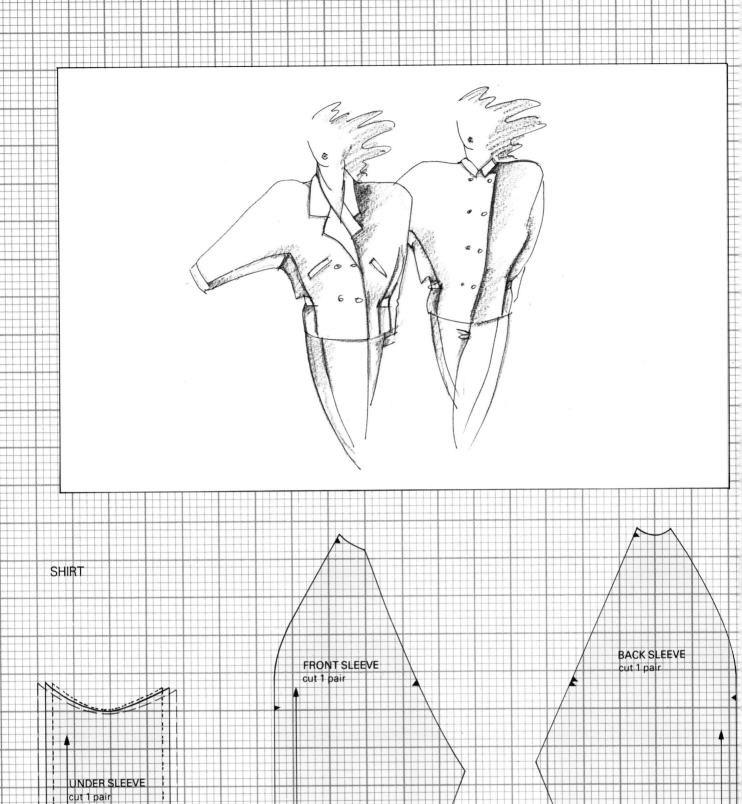

SHIRT

FRONT SLEEVE
cut 1 pair

BACK SLEEVE
cut 1 pair

UNDER SLEEVE
cut 1 pair

pleat

pleat

split

pleat

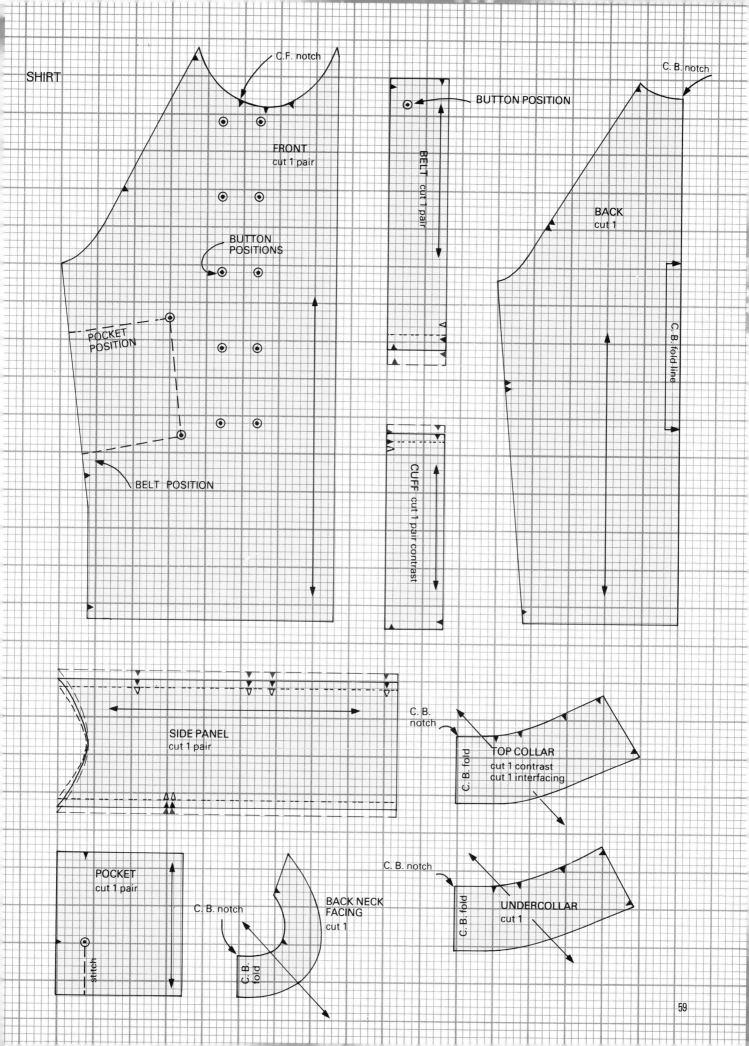

SHIRT

FRONT
cut 1 pair

C.F. notch

BUTTON
POSITIONS

POCKET
POSITION

BELT POSITION

BUTTON POSITION

BELT cut 1 pair

CUFF cut 1 pair contrast

C. B. notch

BACK
cut 1

C. B. fold line

SIDE PANEL
cut 1 pair

C. B.
notch

TOP COLLAR
cut 1 contrast
cut 1 interfacing

C. B. fold

POCKET
cut 1 pair

stitch

C. B. notch

BACK NECK
FACING
cut 1

C. B.
fold

C. B. notch

UNDERCOLLAR
cut 1

C. B. fold

59

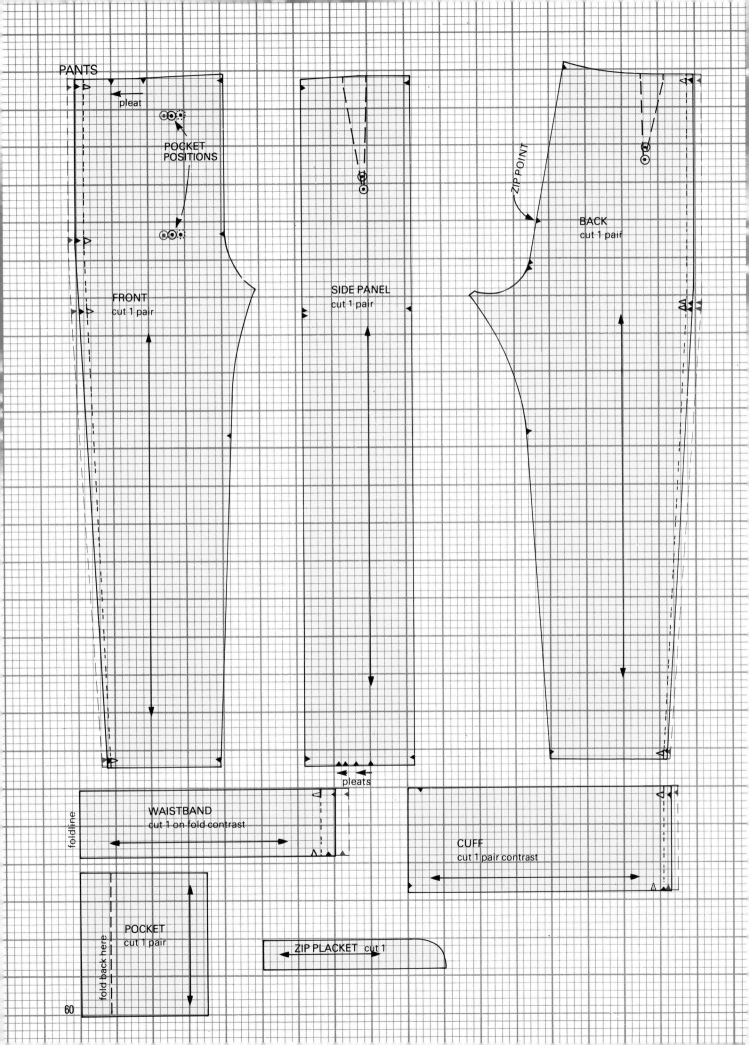

PANTS

POCKET
POSITIONS

pleat

FRONT
cut 1 pair

SIDE PANEL
cut 1 pair

ZIP POINT

BACK
cut 1 pair

pleats

foldline

WAISTBAND
cut 1 on fold contrast

CUFF
cut 1 pair contrast

fold back here

POCKET
cut 1 pair

ZIP PLACKET   cut 1

60

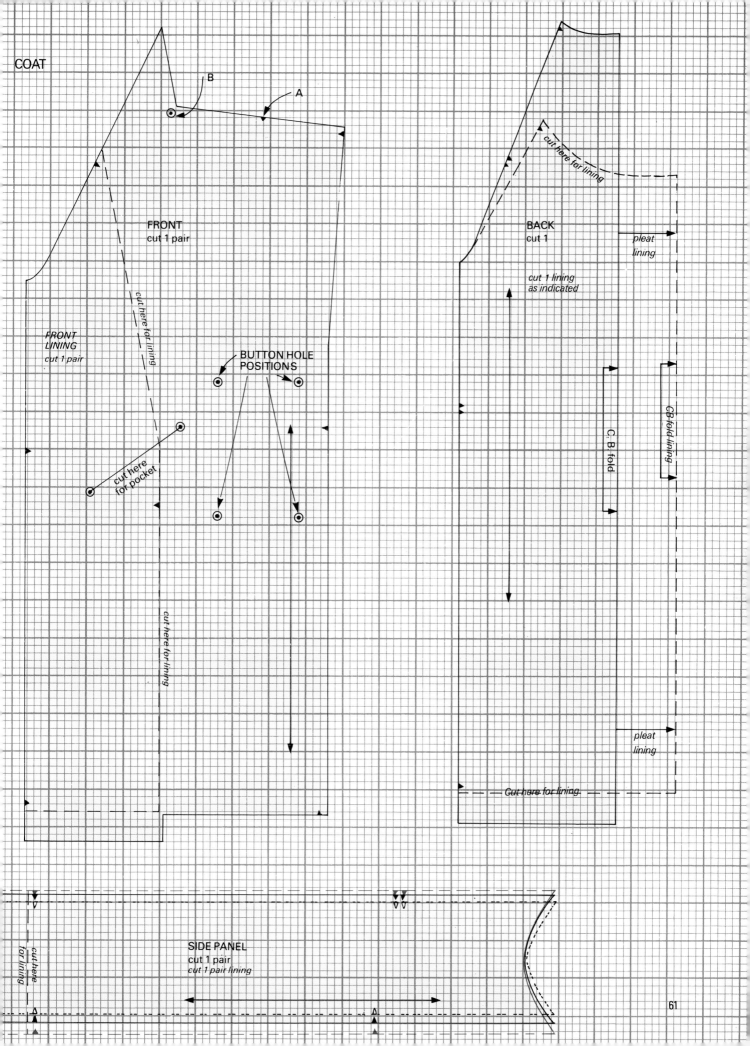

COAT

FRONT
cut 1 pair

B

A

FRONT
LINING
cut 1 pair

cut here for lining

cut here
for pocket

BUTTON HOLE
POSITIONS

cut here for lining

BACK
cut 1

cut here for lining

pleat
lining

cut 1 lining
as indicated

C. B. fold

CB fold lining

pleat
lining

Cut here for lining.

SIDE PANEL
cut 1 pair
cut 1 pair lining

cut here
for lining

61

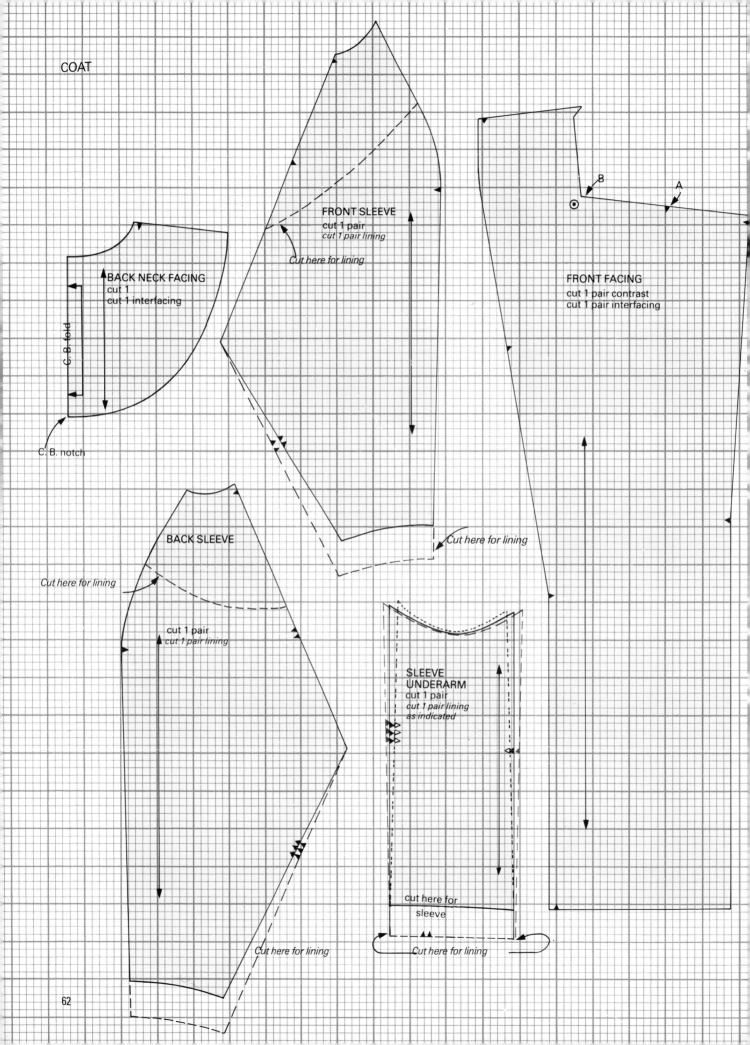

COAT

BACK NECK FACING
cut 1
cut 1 interfacing

C. B. fold

C. B. notch

FRONT SLEEVE
cut 1 pair
cut 1 pair lining

Cut here for lining

FRONT FACING
cut 1 pair contrast
cut 1 pair interfacing

B

A

BACK SLEEVE

Cut here for lining

cut 1 pair
cut 1 pair lining

Cut here for lining

SLEEVE
UNDERARM
cut 1 pair
*cut 1 pair lining
as indicated*

cut here for
sleeve

Cut here for lining

62

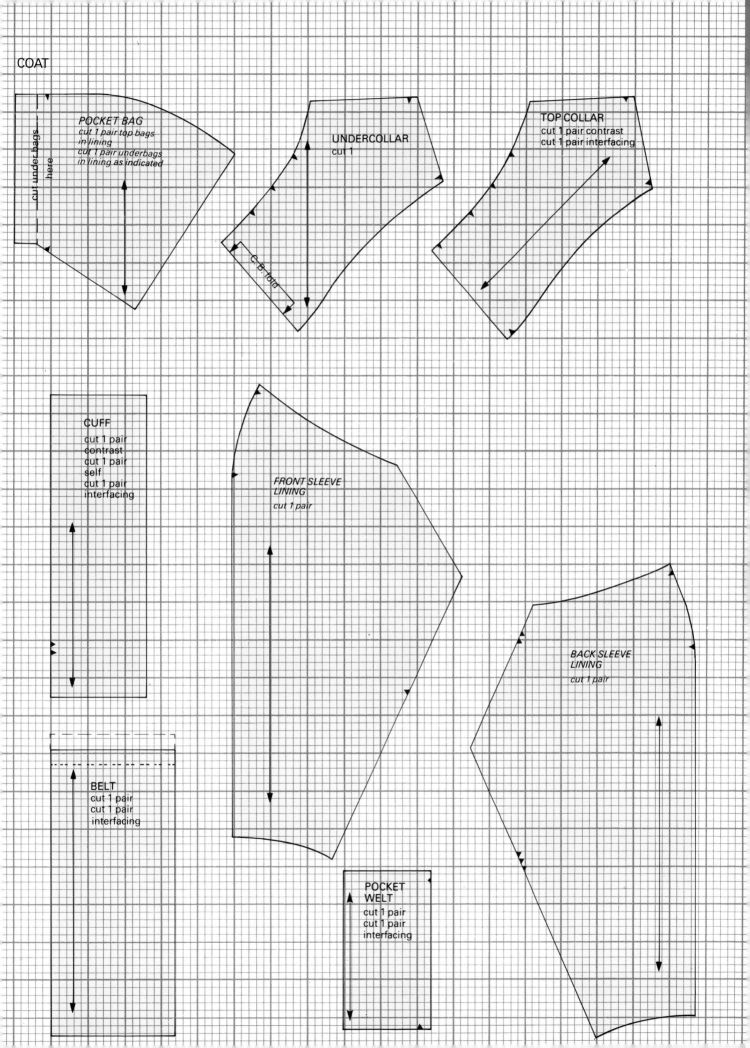

COAT

POCKET BAG
cut 1 pair top bags
in lining
cut 1 pair underbags
in lining as indicated

cut underbags
here

UNDERCOLLAR
cut 1

C.B. fold

TOP COLLAR
cut 1 pair contrast
cut 1 pair interfacing

CUFF

cut 1 pair
contrast
cut 1 pair
self
cut 1 pair
interfacing

FRONT SLEEVE
LINING
cut 1 pair

BACK SLEEVE
LINING
cut 1 pair

BELT
cut 1 pair
cut 1 pair
interfacing

POCKET
WELT
cut 1 pair
cut 1 pair
interfacing

The real starting point for these cool and loosely comfortable layered clothes was a real find in material terms: a beautiful, finely woven, pale blue linen. Since the original objective had been to create a collection that could be thrown on and worn throughout the day, this fabric proved to be the perfect choice, as its habit of creasing and yet still looking good is an inherent part of its charm. Cutting the main pieces into panels and adding interest with a curved line from underarm to cuff produced the strong clean lines envisaged; leaving the neckline plain and uncluttered and making the buttoning as simple as possible reinforced the original design concept – limitation in design is often the best approach. All the individual pieces relate in cut and stitching detail, and there is an optional hip tie on the vest which offers a draped effect.

Summer Breeze

W R A P O V E R   S K I R T

YOU WILL NEED

1.50m of 115cm wide fabric
(or 3.30m of 95cm wide fabric)
4 buttons
2 smaller buttons (for wrong side of wrapover)

The skirt pictured here is set onto a hip basque – flattering to virtually every figure type. It also wraps over at its centre front panel and is complemented at the back with soft unpressed pleats. Pockets are set into the side panels. Fastened at the front with four buttons, the skirt features the same design details as the other garments in this section.

▶1   Join centre back panel to two side panels, right sides together, and stitch from top to bottom. Neaten seam allowances together and press towards centre back, then edgestitch and topstitch 5mm in from edge, machining down length of centre back panel and through seam allowances, on each side.

▶2   Make pleats in back skirt as shown on your pattern, facing them towards sideseams, and staystitch across to hold. Set aside.

▶3   Attach pockets as for Summer Breeze Overshirt, Step 2, neatening, pressing, edge-stitching and topstitching as described. At each remaining raw facing edge, turn under 5mm to wrong side and stitch from top to bottom. Turn in again by 1cm and on wrong side, stitch close to inner folded edge, through all layers to right side. With right side uppermost, edgestitch down folded edge and repeat for other front facing edge. Make pleats as for back in both front side panels: staystitch across to hold.

▶4   Attach one back hip basque to back skirt, stitch from sideseam to sideseam and press seam allowances upwards. Attach front basque in exactly the same way and press seam allowances upwards.

▶5   Join back skirt to front skirts at sideseams, stitching from waist to hem. Neaten seam allowances together from hip basque to hem, pressing towards back, then edgestitch and topstitch 5mm in from edge, machining down length of back skirt at side seams, through seam allowances.

▶6   Make up hip basque facings by attaching second back piece to two front pieces at side seams, right sides together and stitching. Press seam allowances open, then attach to hip basque all the way round, matching notches and sideseams. Stitch across short front basque openings, then around length of waistline to finish at same point at lower front basque opening. Clip corners and curves and turn so that right sides of skirt and facing are uppermost (see Fig.1). On facing, edgestitch all around waistline, beginning and ending 4cm in from each front opening edge, through seam allowances. Neaten lower raw edge of facing.

▶7   Turn facing to inside and press all round. Laying skirt on ironing board, set facing flat against hip basque, underlapping skirt's lower neatened edge by its seam allowance. Then, working from right side edge, topstitch 5mm in from edge, along lower edge of basque, through seam allowances and facings. Press.

▶8   To finish hemline, decide on length, then turn up 5mm to wrong side and stitch all round from front opening to front opening. Turn up 1cm again to wrong side and edgestitch around inner folded edge, through to right side. Turn to right side and edgestitch again all the way round, close to lower folded edge of skirt. Press.

▶9   Make buttonholes and attach buttons as marked on your pattern, and attach narrow hanging loops by hand to underside of facing at each sideseam.

fig.1

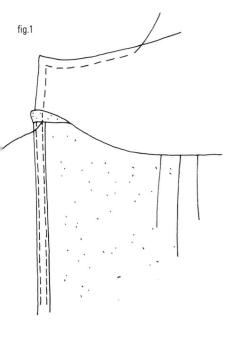

Summer Breeze
P A N T S

YOU WILL NEED

2m of 115cm wide fabric
(or 2.65m of 95cm wide fabric)
1 zip, 20cm long

These loose pants, cropped off just above the ankles, have soft, unpressed pleats, making them extremely easy to wear. Like the skirt, they are set onto a hip basque, with roomy practical prockets, but a zip set into the side seam.

▶1   Make darts in back pants, stitch and press towards sideseams. Set front double pleats as marked on your pattern, facing them towards each side seam, and staystich across to hold. Attach half pocket bags to front sideseams, right sides together, and matching notch to top of pocket bag. Stitch from top to bottom and press seam allowances open. Repeat for back pocket bags, pressing allowances towards hip edge.

▶2   Attach back inside leg to front inside leg, right sides together, and stitch. Repeat for other leg, then neaten seam allowances separately and press open. Join pants at top centre front point, right sides together; pin all round crutch curve, finishing at top centre back point. Stitch all round, then stitch again 2mm outside original stitching line to strengthen. Trim back seam allowances to 1cm and press open.

▶3   Attach one back hip basque to back pants, right sides together, and stitch across. Repeat for front hip basque. Press both seam allowances upwards towards waist. Turn pants so that right sides of side seams come together, then stitch down right side seam from top to bottom. Stitch down left sideseam to hem, 1cm above raw top of pocket. Neaten seam allowances together and press towards front. On right side of front pants, edgestitch and topstitch 5mm in from edge of sideseams, through seam allowances, from top to beginning of pocket. Pivot needle, stitch horizontally 5mm in towards centre front, pivot needle again and return to top, topstitching 5mm in from edge. Repeat this stitching detail, beginning at hem and working up into pants to pocket opening, then down again to hem. Repeat for left sideseam, but from hem to pocket opening only.

▶4   Press zip opening seam allowance back onto wrong side, then set in zip as marked on your pattern. Stitch by machine or insert by hand, using a stabstitch. Press carefully.

▶5   Prepare hip basque facing by joining right sides together at right sideseam only. Stitch, press seam allowance open, then set against hip basque, right sides together and matching left sideseam and centre front and centre back notches. Folding back zip seam allowance to wrong side, stitch all round and turn so that pants and facing are uppermost. Then edgestitch around facing and through seam allowances. Neaten remaining raw edge of facing, turn to wrong side and set into position, pinning flat behind hip basque so that it underlaps the original stitching line by its seam allowance, and tucking in seam allowance on zip side to the wrong side. Slipstitch down zip opening facing on each side to secure them on right side, then edgestitch and topstitch 5mm in from edge, working all round lower edge of hip basque, from zip to zip, and through hip basque facing.

▶6   To finish hems, decide on length, and, working from wrong side, turn in by 5mm and stitch all round. Make a second 1cm turning and edgestitch round inner folded edge, through to right side. Turn to right side and edgestitch around lower folded edge of each ankle. Press pants to finish.

Summer Breeze
D U S T E R   C O A T

YOU WILL NEED

4.60m of 95cm wide fabric
5 buttons
1 pair shoulder pads (curved)

A generously cut, casual duster coat which can be made to any length. It incorporates pockets and interesting cutting detail in underarm panels as well as topstitched detailing.

▶1   Join two back pieces of coat at centre back, right sides together, stitch, neaten seam allowances together and press towards right back. On right side, edgestitch and topstitch 5mm in from edge on right back, machining through seam allowances and working from the top to the bottom.

69

▶2 Join front to back at shoulder seams, right sides together, and stitch. Neaten seam allowances together and press towards back. With right side uppermost, edgestitch and topstitch 5mm in from edge, through seam allowances, from neck to cuff edge on coat back. Attach one half pocket bag to each front sideseam's extended 'ear pieces', matching notches; stitch from top to bottom. Press towards outside and set aside.

▶3 Join long side panels to shorter underarm panels at underarm seamline, right sides together; stitch across. Neaten seam allowances together and press towards arm. Join two side and arm panels together at side seams (i.e. the shorter of the two long sides of these joined side panels), matching notches; stitch from cuff to hem. Neaten seam allowances together and press towards back, then repeat for other side. Edgestitch and topstitch each completed side panel on right side, through seam allowances, and working from cuff to hem. Repeat edgestitching and topstitching, machining 5mm in from edge on underarm seamlines of both side panels.

▶4 Join each side panel to back of jacket, right sides together and matching underarm notch to underarm seamline of side panel. Neaten each seam allowance together and press towards centre back, then on right side, edgestitch and topstitch 5mm in from edge around coat back, machining through seam allowances on each side and working from cuff to hem.

▶5 Attach pocket bags to side panels, right sides together and matching notches, with the greater part of each pocket above each notch; stitch from top to bottom. Press seam allowances open, then attach front to side panel at each side, right sides together; starting at cuff, pin all the way down, down and around pocket bag, to finish at hemline. Then stitch up seamline from bottom inner corner of pocket bag to notch point on seam allowance 6cm up, keeping all seam allowances clear. Neaten seam allowances and press towards centre front. Now edgestitch up to pocket opening through seam allowances and then, pivoting needle in fabric, stitch horizontally towards centre front for just 5mm. Pivot needle again and topstitching 5mm in from edge,

return to hem. Repeat this operation for seamline above pocket and extending to cuff, on each side of coat.

▶6 Join back neck facing to front neck facings at shoulder seams, right sides together, and stitch across. Press seam allowances open, then lay back neck facing against back neck, right sides together and matching shoulder seamlines. Pin, and set foldback point of front opening on each front coat piece, matching centre front notches. Stitch all round, then repeat complete stitching line again for strength, stitching 1–2mm inside original stitching line; clip curves. Turn so that both coat and facing are right sides uppermost, then edgestitch around neckline curve on facing, through seam allowances, from 3cm each side of front opening. Turn facing to wrong side and press.

▶7 Neaten inner raw edge of front and back facing by turning 5mm to wrong side and stitching all round. Finish hem by turning front facings back onto right side of coat, matching centre front notches; stitch across facings at hemline. Turn 5mm to wrong side around remaining hemline and stitch. Turn 1cm again to wrong side and edgestitch on inside of coat, close to inner folded edge; machine all the way round and through to right side, starting and finishing at front opening of coat. On right side, edgestitch all the way round bottom of coat to create a double line of stitching, as before.

▶8 Repeat this finishing operation in exactly the same way as described for cuffs. To finish neckline, edgestitch all around neck edge, from front opening to front opening, then topstitch again 5mm in from edge all the way round so that the same stitching effect as on the hem is achieved. Press carefully, basting down front openings if necessary to achieve a straight pressing line. Make buttonholes and attach buttons as marked on your pattern. Finally slipstitch facing to pocket seam allowance to hold in place.

▶9 To make up one pair of shoulder pad covers, lay a shoulder pad on fabric and cut round its shape, allowing 1cm extra all round as a seam allowance. Cut two pairs, then stitch all round one pair, right sides together, leaving a gap through which to turn the cover. Trim corners, turn and insert a pad into the cover so that it lies flat inside, then close opening with a few slipstitches. Repeat for other pad. Attach finished pads to inside of shoulder seam allowance so that the wide end of each pad slightly overlaps your natural shoulder edge. Attach with loose handstitches at narrow and wide end of each pad to secure in place.

The little vest top shown here follows the same design lines as the other clothes in this section. It is shaped loosely, to be worn either plain or with the optional hip ties which attach to the centre back panel.

Summer Breeze
VEST TOP

YOU WILL NEED

1.35m of 115cm wide fabric
(or 1.80m of 95cm wide fabric)

▶1 Make up hip ties by first folding each tie in half lengthways, right sides together. Stitch along long raw edge and up unnotched short end, then trim corners and turn to right side. Press. Pleat remaining raw short end of each tie as notched (see Fig.1), pleating downwards. Stay-stitch across pleats, then set against centre back panel so that raw edges align, remembering that the longer tie is set against the right back of the centre back panel as you look at it. Staystitch each side.

▶2 Attach centre back panel to both side panels, sandwiching hip ties inbetween; stitch from top to bottom. Trim tie seam allowances, then neaten seam allowances together, pressing towards centre back. On right side, edgestitch and topstitch 5mm in from edge on each side of centre back panel, from top to bottom and through seam allowances. Make up front bodice as above but omitting hip tie instructions. Press front and back bodice.

▶3 Join front to back bodice at side seams, right sides together. Stitch, neaten seam allowances together and press towards centre front.

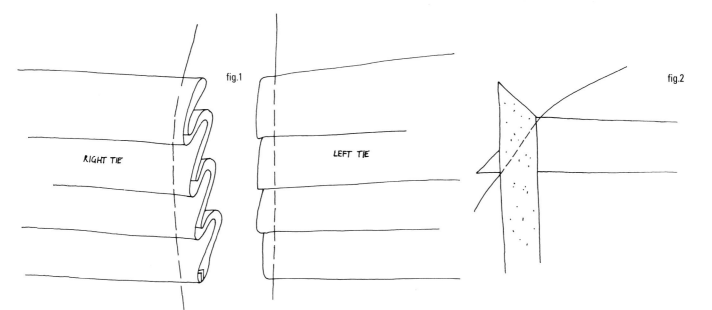

fig.1 RIGHT TIE LEFT TIE fig.2

On right side, edgestitch and topstitch 5mm in from edge, machining down front bodice and through seam allowances. Repeat for shoulder seams, again pressing seam allowances towards front.

▶4   Stitch together strips of binding as shown in Fig.2, to make one long length; press seam allowances open. To bind neck edge, start at a shoulder seamline and pin right side of binding to right side of neck edge, folding binding back on itself at short end (illustrated in Fig.3) to neaten, and matching raw edges. Trim off end of binding, allowing a 1.5cm overlap, then stitch all round. Turn top so that right sides of bodice and binding are uppermost, and seam allowances face towards edge of binding. Edgestitch all round binding, through seam allowances, and close to first line of stitching. Clip curves, then turn facing to inside and turn under by 5mm. Edgestitch all round inner folded edge of binding, machining through to right side. On right side of top, edgestitch around neck opening edge and press.

▶5   Repeat this method of binding for both armhole openings, beginning at underarm points. Press completed top carefully.

fig.3

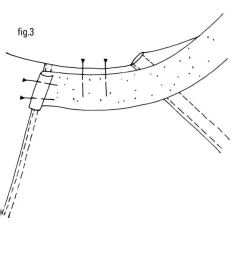

O V E R S H I R T

A comfortably cut, very wearable overshirt to team with the matching skirt or pants, as shown here. Alternatively it could be lengthened into a dress to be worn belted or straight. The shirt's design lines match those of the other garments in this section: interesting front and back panels, pockets and topstitched detail.

▶1   Join centre back panel to two side back panels, right sides together and matching notches. Stitch from top to bottom, then press seam allowances towards centre back. Working from right side and from neck to hem, edgestitch and topstitch 5mm in from edge on centre back panel, through seam allowances.

▶2   Attach a half pocket bag to each centre front panel, right sides together and matching notches, with the greater part of each pocket above the notch; stitch from top to bottom. Press seam allowances open, then attach a full pocket bag to each side front panel as before, right sides together, and keeping the larger part of each pocket bag above the notch marked. Stitch from top to bottom and then press seam allowances towards outside. Next attach centre front panels to side front panels, matching notches and pocket bags; stitch from top to bottom, machining around pocket bag on each side. Press seam allowances towards centre front, then stitch up seamline from bottom inner corner of pocket bag to notch point marked 6cm above on seam allowance, keeping all seam allowances clear. Neaten seam allowances together and press towards centre front. On right side, edgestitch up to pocket opening from bottom, machining through seam allowances, and pivoting needle in fabric to stitch horizontally outwards towards centre front for just 5mm. Pivot needle again, and topstitching 5mm in from edge, return to hem. Repeat for seamline above pocket opening and up to shoulder line. Repeat for other side of front.

▶3   Attach front to back shirt at shoulder seam, right sides together and matching notches, stitching from neck to cuff. Neaten seam allowances and press towards back. Then on right side, edgestitch and topstitch 5mm in from

edge on back sleeve, through all seam allowances, from neck to cuff. Repeat for other side.

▶4   Attach back neck facing to front facings at shoulderlines, right sides together, and stitch across. Trim back neck facing seam allowance only, then press seam allowances towards back, folding back each front facing to lie flat against neckline and so that centre front notches meet. Continue to attach facing to neck edge, right sides together, all the way round, stitching from front opening to front opening. Clip curves, turn so that right sides of both shirt and facing are uppermost, then edgestitch along facing and through seam allowances, from about 4cm from front opening, to finish at the same point on other side of neckline. Press.

▶5   Trim off remaining inner front facing edge at pocket 'ear' point, then neaten all round inner raw front and back facing edges, working from hem to hem. Fold hem of facing back on itself to fold at notch point marked on the pattern, then stitch across hemline, 1.5cm up from raw edge. Trim, turn to right side and then, laying each front section flat on ironing board, wrong side uppermost, set facings against shirt so that facing inner seam allowance overlaps seamline by 1.5cm (see Fig.1). Pin, then on right side, edgestitch down centre front panel, through underpinned facing to pocket opening. Pivot needle and stitch horizontally inwards for exactly 5mm. Pivot needle again, and then topstitch 5mm in from edge, up to starting point at shoulder line. Repeat for other side and press. Turning shirt upside down, repeat edgestitching and topstitching on each side of front panels, working from hem to bottom of pocket opening and down again. Press.

▶6   Join both sideseams of shirt, right sides together and matching notches; stitch from cuff to hem. Neaten seam allowances together and press towards back. Repeat edgestitching and topstitching detail from each cuff right the way through to hemline and press.

▶7   To finish hem, turn 5mm to inside at lower raw edge of hem and stitch. Turn 1cm again to inside, pin, then edgestitch all round hem, machining close to inner folded edge of hem. On right side, edgestitch again from facing stitching line to facing stitching line, close to lower edge of hem. Repeat for each cuff edge; press finished garment carefully.

▶8   Attach buttons and make buttonholes as marked on your pattern.

fig.1

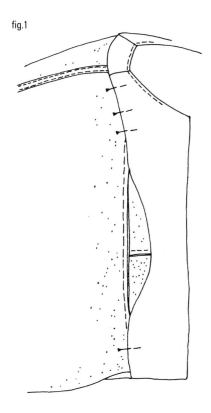

SKIRT

For key to symbols see page nine

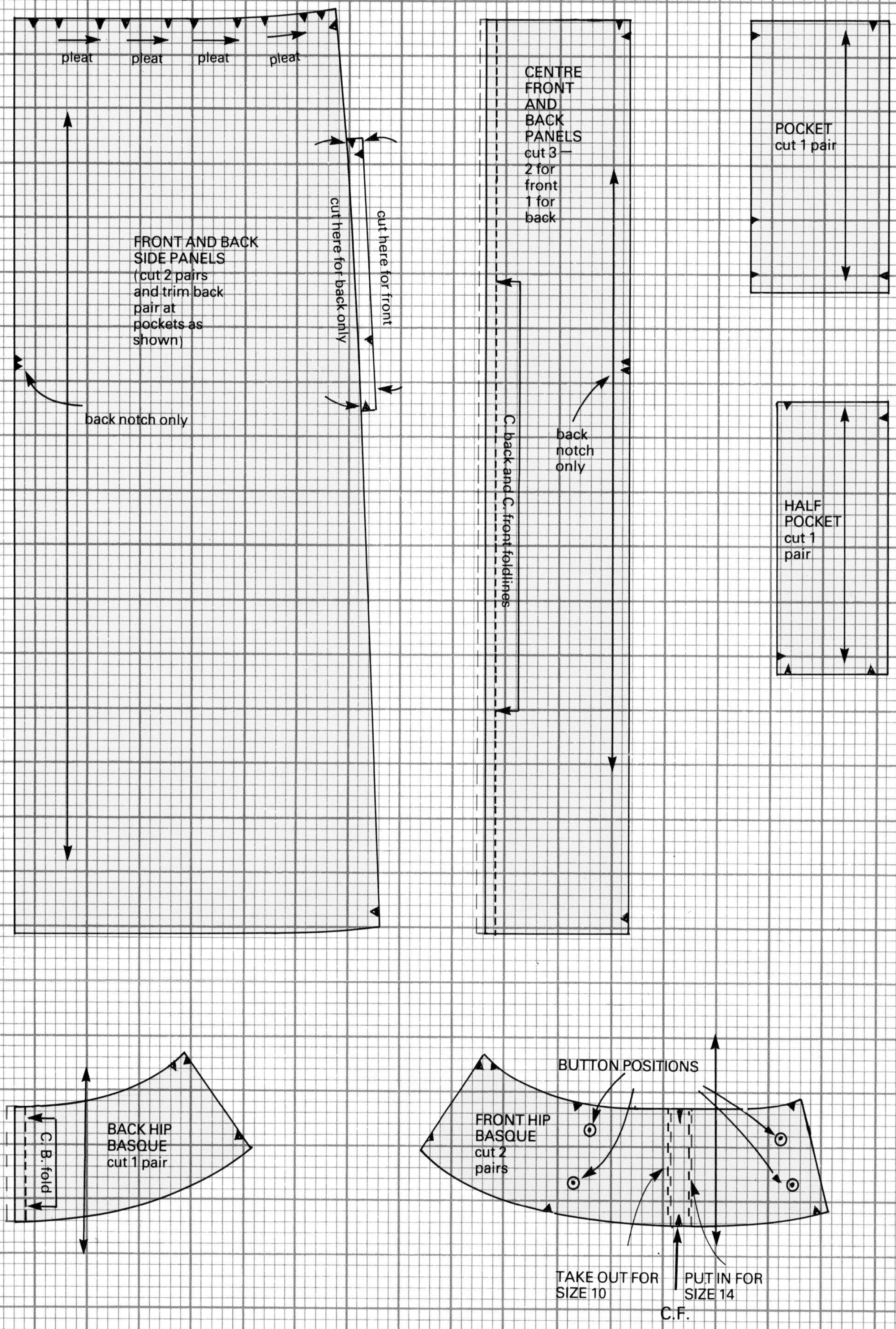

FRONT AND BACK SIDE PANELS
(cut 2 pairs and trim back pair at pockets as shown)

pleat   pleat   pleat   pleat

cut here for back only

cut here for front

back notch only

CENTRE FRONT AND BACK PANELS
cut 3 —
2 for front
1 for back

back notch only

C. back and C. front foldlines

POCKET
cut 1 pair

HALF POCKET
cut 1 pair

BACK HIP BASQUE
cut 1 pair

C. B. fold

FRONT HIP BASQUE
cut 2 pairs

BUTTON POSITIONS

TAKE OUT FOR SIZE 10

PUT IN FOR SIZE 14

C.F.

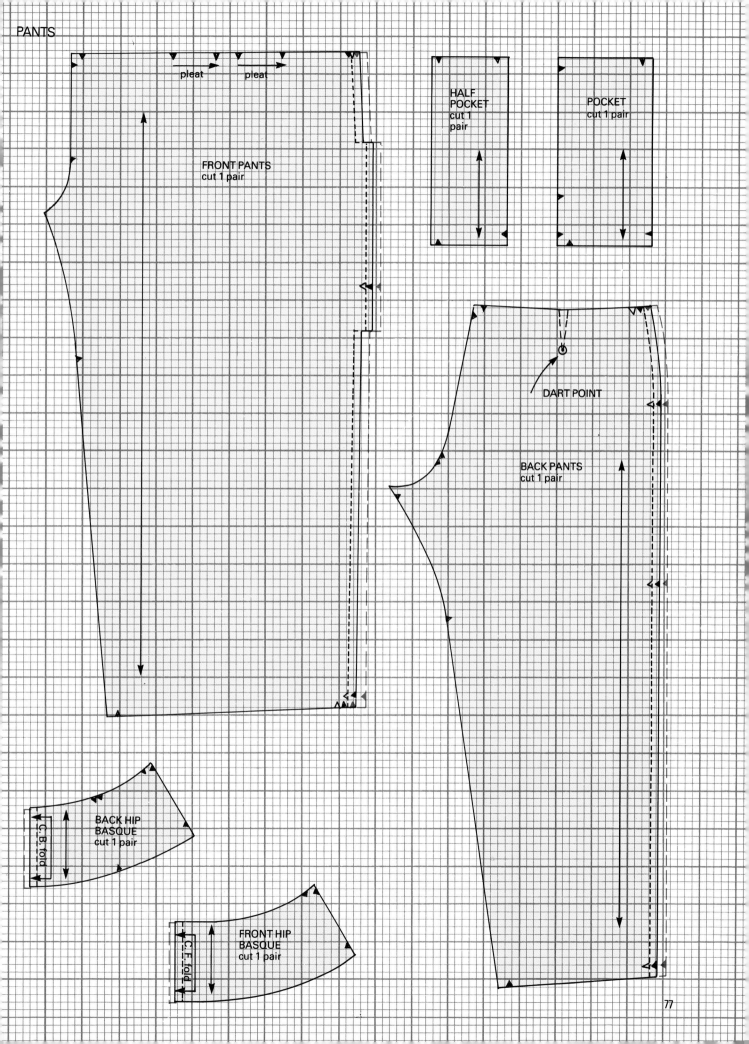

PANTS

FRONT PANTS
cut 1 pair

pleat   pleat

HALF
POCKET
cut 1
pair

POCKET
cut 1 pair

DART POINT

BACK PANTS
cut 1 pair

BACK HIP
BASQUE
cut 1 pair

C. B. fold

FRONT HIP
BASQUE
cut 1 pair

C. F. fold

77

COAT

FRONT COAT
cut 1 pair

BUTTON
POSITIONS

foldline

POCKET POSITION

HALF
POCKET
BAG
cut 1 pair

FRONT AND
BACK
SIDE
PANELS
cut
2 pairs

POCKET
BAG
cut 1 pair

PUT IN FOR SIZE 14   TAKE OUT FOR SIZE 10

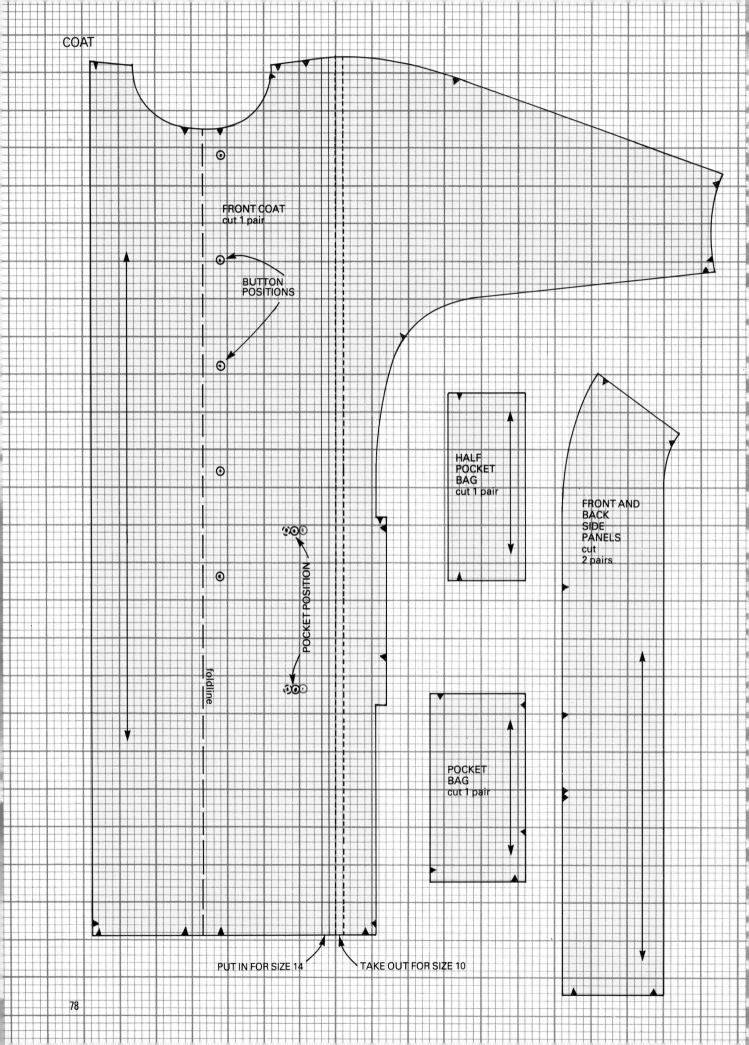

COAT

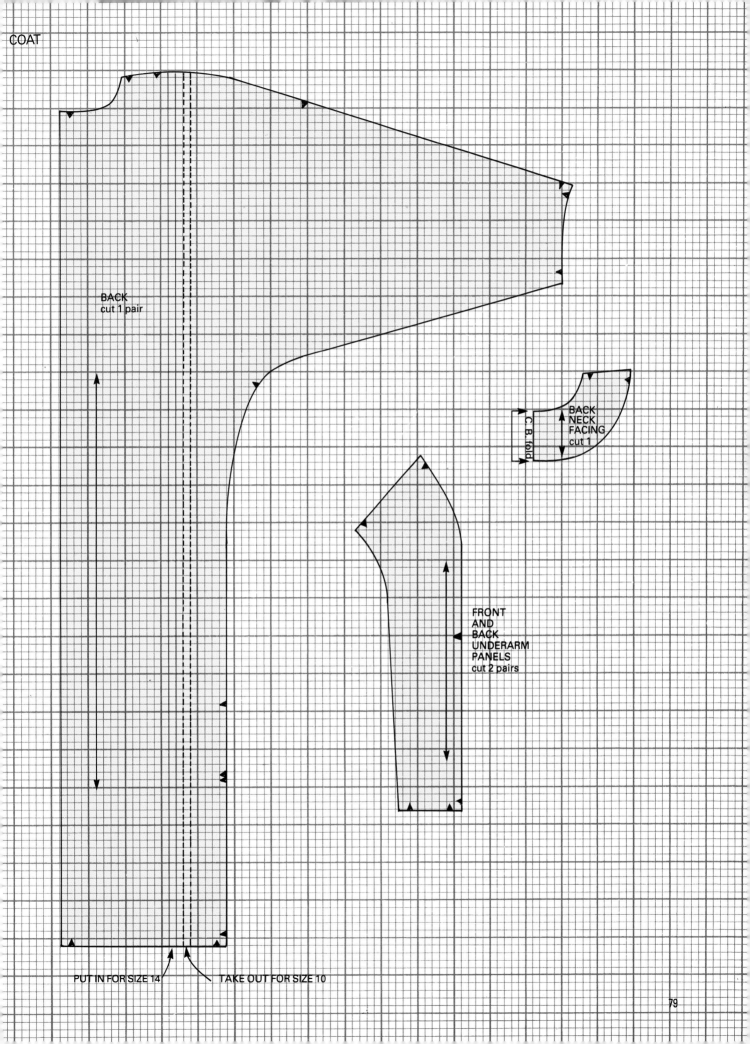

BACK
cut 1 pair

BACK
NECK
FACING
cut 1

C. B. fold

FRONT
AND
BACK
UNDERARM
PANELS
cut 2 pairs

PUT IN FOR SIZE 14   TAKE OUT FOR SIZE 10

79

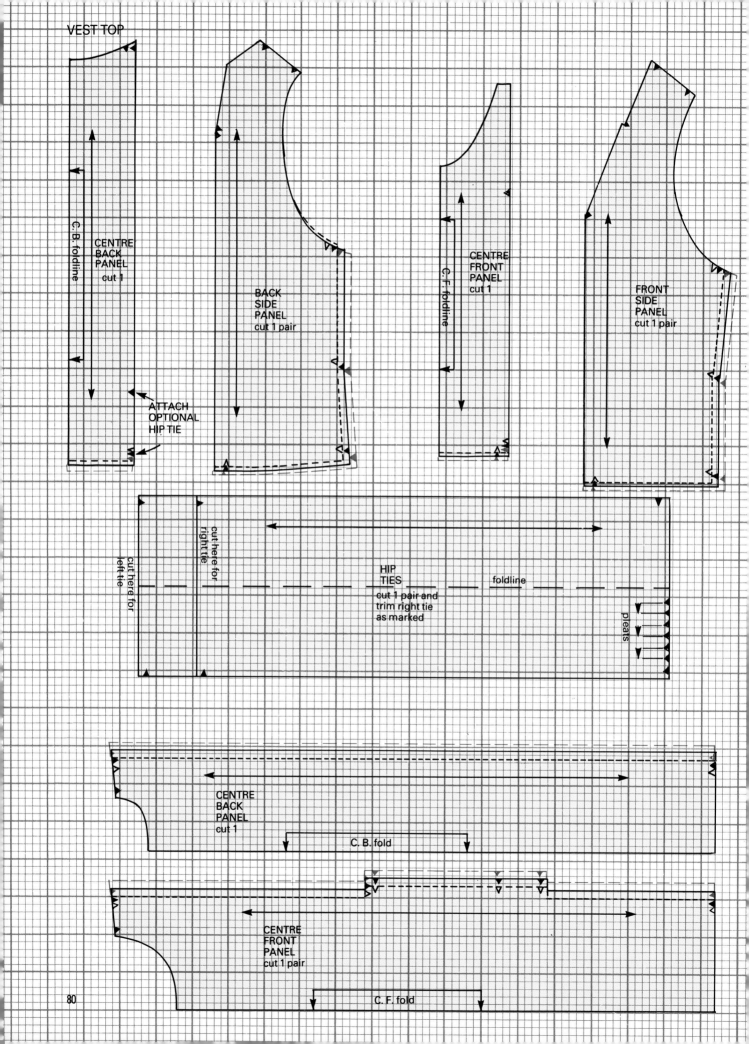

VEST TOP

CENTRE
BACK
PANEL
cut 1

C. B. foldline

ATTACH
OPTIONAL
HIP TIE

BACK
SIDE
PANEL
cut 1 pair

CENTRE
FRONT
PANEL
cut 1

C. F. foldline

FRONT
SIDE
PANEL
cut 1 pair

cut here for
right tie

cut here for
left tie

HIP
TIES
cut 1 pair and
trim right tie
as marked

foldline

pleats

CENTRE
BACK
PANEL
cut 1

C. B. fold

CENTRE
FRONT
PANEL
cut 1 pair

C. F. fold

OVERSHIRT

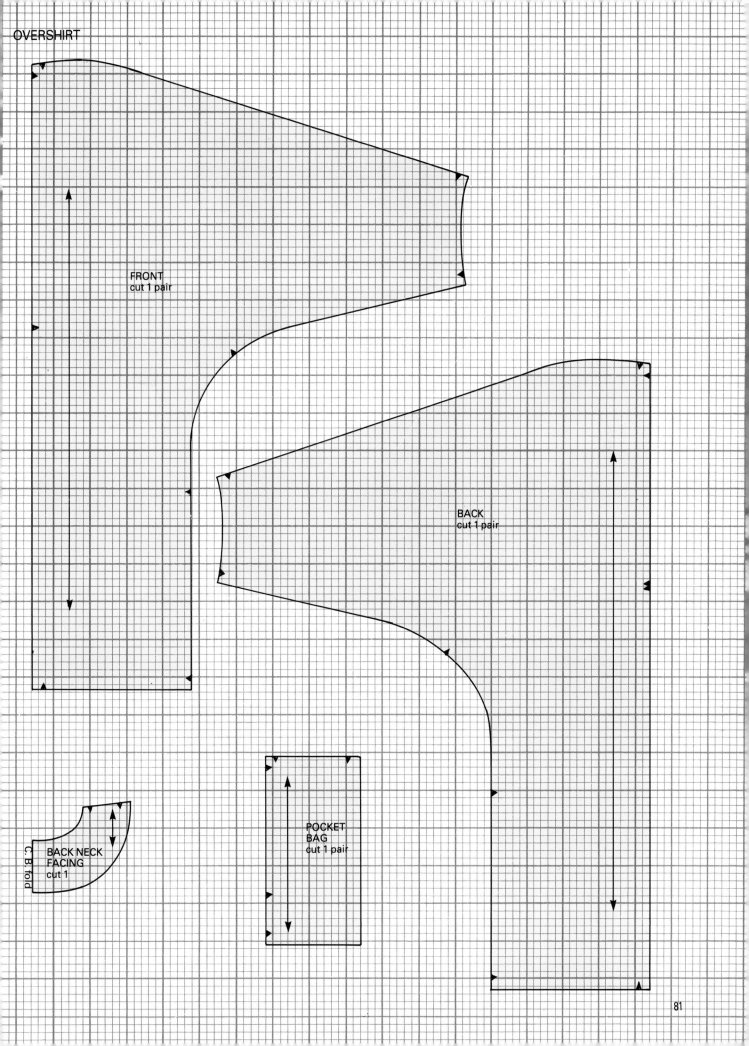

FRONT
cut 1 pair

BACK
cut 1 pair

C. B. fold

BACK NECK
FACING
cut 1

POCKET
BAG
cut 1 pair

This collection owes much to the 'Sixties', when lines were neat and severe, and skirts were often incredibly short! The objective, therefore, was a simple, uncluttered look – a number of close-to-the-body separates that offer a dressed up feel, but which are also young looking and very easy to make. Design detail has been added by incorporating double-breasted buttoning, with a line that runs through the pants, skirt and dress. There is even a Chanel-style collar on the dress and blouse, that stands away to frame the face in a softly flattering way. The use of strongly coloured polycotton gaberdine strengthens the feeling of youth and freshness and means the more fitted garments can be worn in several different combinations, with lots of potential for contrast fabric features.

Streets Ahead

Streets Ahead
D R E S S

This neat little semi-fitted dress has a centre front panel highlighted with four buttons. The zip is hidden away centre back and the hemline falls just above the knee. The soft, stand-away collar looks good made in a contrast fabric to match the jacket.

▶1   To make up back dress, begin by setting darts in back dress pieces and then stitch; press seam allowances towards sideseams. Join two back pieces at centre back seamline and stitch from notch marking bottom of zip to hemline. Neaten seam allowances separately from neck to hem, then baste from neck to zip notch; sew down centre back seamline, pressing seam allowances open. Set zip into place directly behind centre back basting, beginning 1cm down from top raw edge of neck. Stitch in place or insert by hand using stabstitch.

▶2   To make up front dress, set bust and waist darts in two side front dress pieces. Stitch, then press bust darts downwards and waist darts towards sideseams. Set centre front dress panel against two side front dress pieces, right sides together and matching notches; stitch from top to bottom down each side. Neaten seam allowances together and press towards centre front. On right side, edgestitch down each side of front panel, machining close to original line of stitching and through seam allowances. Press.

▶3   Join front to back dress at shoulders and sideseams, right sides together; stitch. Neaten all seam allowances separately, then press open.

▶4   Make up collar by setting top collar against undercollar piece, right sides together, and stitching around long outer curved edge and two short edges. Trim corners, turn and press. Repeat for other collar piece, then roll each piece over your hand so that the top collar is uppermost and the whole collar has a natural curve or fall to it. (See Fig.1.) You will find that the undercollar juts out beyond the top collar raw edge by 5mm. Baste these raw edges into position to set. Repeat for other side.

▶5   Attach collar pieces to raw neck edge, undercollar to right side of neck edge, matching notches, and aligning the longer of each short edge of collar pieces to the centre front point of the dress. The shorter of these two short collar

edges will then align with the centre back opening. Baste and set aside.

▶6   Make up facing by attaching two back facing pieces to front facing pieces at shoulders and underarms. Stitch, then press seam allowances open. Neaten lower continuing edge of facing from centre back to centre back point. Attach facing at neck, right side to top collar, and stitch all round; fold centre back facing seam allowances back to inside to neaten as shown in Fig.2. Clip curves of neckline seam allowances, then turn neckline so that right sides of facing and collars are uppermost; edgestitch along facing, close to first line of stitching joining collar, and machining from centre back to centre back point.

▶7   To finish armholes, turn under 1cm all round armhole opening and baste close to folded edge. Repeat for armhole facing, then set together with folds facing to the inside, matching shoulder and underarm seamlines; edgestitch close to folded edges, all the way round armhole opening. Turning to the wrong side, clip seam allowances evenly all around curved edges, then press carefully. Repeat for other armhole. Attach underarm facing to dress side seam allowances on the inside of the dress at its lowest edge, sewing by hand. Slipstitch facing foldbacks flat against the edge of the zip at centre back opening.

▶8   Neaten raw hem edge all round, then turn up as notched and slipstitch all the way round hem by hand. Lastly, attach four buttons as marked on your pattern to the centre front panel.

YOU WILL NEED
2.25m of 115cm wide fabric
30cm of 115cm wide fabric (contrast)
1 zip, 55cm long
4 buttons

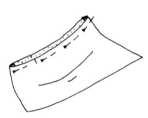

fig.1

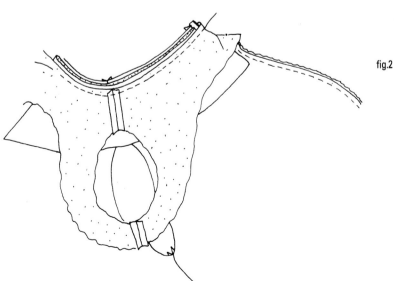

fig.2

Streets Ahead
S K I R T

A simple skirt with a front panel, repeating the lines of the jacket and blouse. The garment also features hip pockets, centre back zip fastening, and a hemline turned up to just above the knee.

▶1   Make darts in both back skirt pieces; stitch and press towards side seams.

▶2   Join centre back seam of back skirt pieces, right sides together; stitch from notch marking bottom of zip to hem. Baste from zip notch to waist, then neaten seam allowances separately and press open. Set zip directly behind centre back basted seamline, beginning 1cm down from raw edge of waistline; insert in place either by machine or by hand, using a stabstitch.

▶3   Attach a half pocket bag to each side front skirt piece, right sides together and matching notches. Stitch across top, on each side. Turn so that both half pocket bag and front skirt are uppermost, then edgestitch along pocket bag close to first line of stitching and through seam allowances. Press each half pocket bag to the wrong side of side front skirt pieces.

▶4 With wrong side of each side front skirt piece uppermost, set a pocket back against each half pocket bag, right sides downwards, matching notches; stitch across bottom of each pocket only. Neaten seam allowances together, then staystitch up each side of each pocket, 1cm in from raw edges.

▶5 Attach centre front panel to each side front skirt piece, right sides together and matching notches. Stitch down both sides from top to bottom, neaten seam allowances together and press towards centre front. On right side of skirt, edgestitch down each side of centre front panel and through seam allowances, machining from top to bottom.

▶6 Attach back to front skirt at sideseams, right sides together and matching notches. Stitch from top to bottom down each side, neaten seam allowances separately and press open.

▶7 To attach waistband, start by running a line of basting stitches between back dart and centre front panel, around waistline. Now set waistband

into position, right sides together and with right back extension of waistband overlapping zip as notched. Pin into position, easing around basting lines, then stitch all round waistline. Fold waistband in half lengthways so that right sides come together, and stitch across extension end and along its lower side to finish at centre back opening. Trim corner and turn extension to right side. At other end of waistband, fold again so that right sides come together and stitch across short ends. Trim and turn to right side. Fold 1cm under to wrong side along remaining long raw edge of waistband so that foldline wraps very slightly over original stitching line; pin into position. Then on right side, stitch along join of waistband to skirt and through inside folded edge of waistband, machining from centre back to centre back. Press.

▶8 To finish hem, neaten raw hem edge all the way round, turn up to wrong side as notched on your pattern, and hemstitch all round. Press.

▶9 Make buttonhole and attach button to back waistband opening as marked on your pattern.

Streets Ahead
B L O U S E

A square cut blouse that will happily double as a sleeveless jacket over other garments in the outfit or T-shirts. Note the double-breasted front, patch pockets and sixties-style collar.

▶1 Make darts in back bodice and stitch. Press towards armholes, then make darts in front bodice pieces and stitch. Press downwards.

▶2 Join back bodice to two front bodice pieces at sideseams, right sides together; stitch from underarm to hem on each side. Neaten seam allowances separately and press open. Repeat for shoulder seams, neatening seam allowances separately as before and pressing open.

▶3 Make up collar by setting two collar pieces right sides together, and stitching around outer curved, unnotched edge and two short ends. Trim corners and turn so that right sides of top and undercollar are uppermost. Starting and ending 4cm from each corner, edgestitch along undercollar and through seam allowances, close

to first line of stitching. Press collar flat, then set remaining notched raw edge with your hand positioned beneath undercollar so that it folds naturally back on itself (see Dress, Step 4). You will find that the undercollar juts out by 3mm beneath the top collar, thus allowing top collar to roll naturally over undercollar. Pin, then stay-stitch into position.

▶4 Set undercollar against right side of neckline, matching notches, so that fronts of collar come to centre front bodice notches; pin, then staystitch to hold in place. Attach back neck facing to front facings at shoulderline, right sides together, stitching across. Press seam allowances open. At front foldlines, fold self-facing back on itself, right sides together, then set remainder of facing into position, matching notches. Stitch all round, enclosing collar as in a sandwich. Trim, clip curves and turn so that right sides of top collar and facing are uppermost. Edgestitch along facing from collar edge to collar edge, machining close to first line of stitching and through seam allowances. Turn facing to wrong side and press carefully all around neckline.

YOU WILL NEED

1.40m of 115cm wide fabric
8 buttons

▶5 Join armhole facings at underarm points, right sides together; stitch. Press seam allowances open, then set each facing in place against armhole openings, right sides together and matching notches. Stitch all round, then open out so that right sides of facing and bodice are uppermost. Edgestitch around facing, machining close to first line of stitching and through seam allowances. Clip curves, then neaten inside edge of facing all round and press to inside of bodice. Hemstitch around inside of each armhole facing to hold in place.

▶6 To finish hem, begin by neatening inside neck facing all the way round. Then turn front self-facings back on themselves at hemline as notched, right sides together; stitch across facings, 1.5cm in from raw edges. Neaten remaining hemline, then turning facings back to wrong side, fold up hemline as marked on your

pattern; pin, then hemstitch into place. Next, laying front bodice flat on ironing board, press down foldline at front edges as marked on your pattern. Slipstitch shoulder facings into position against shoulder seamlines to hold.

▶7 To make pockets, neaten top of each pocket and fold back, right sides together, along notch marks showing foldline on your pattern. Stitch down each short side as notched, then turn back to right side. Neaten remaining raw edges of each pocket, and press seam allowances to wrong side around remaining three sides of pocket. Set into position against blouse fronts as marked on your pattern, then edgestitch around three pressed sides of each pocket, leaving the tops open. Press.

▶8 Make buttonholes and attach buttons to front blouse as marked on your pattern.

Streets Ahead
P A N T S

YOU WILL NEED
2.10m of 115cm wide fabric
1 zip, 20cm long
3 buttons

Fitted, ankle-length pants with centre back zip fastening, hip pockets, and an inset front panel that matches the buttoning of the blouse and jacket.

▶1 Make darts in back pants pieces, stitch and press towards sideseams. Join back pants pieces at centre back seamline, right sides together, from notch point marking bottom of zip to crutch. Baste from zip notch to waistline, then neaten seam allowances and press open. Set zip directly behind basted seamline and beginning 1cm down from raw waist edge; insert by machine or by hand, using a stabstitch.

▶2 Attach a half pocket bag to each front pants piece, matching notches. Stitch across top, then turn so that both half pocket bag and pants are right sides uppermost. Edgestitch along half pocket bag close to first line of stitching, machining through seam allowances, on each side. Turn half pocket bags to wrong side of pants pieces and press, then set a pocket back behind each half pocket bag, matching notches. Stitch around bottom and inner side of each pocket, working 1cm in from raw edge and finishing at edge of pocket opening (marked Point A). Neaten curve from Point A down and around bottom of pockets to side seams. Clip seam allowances at Points A to release; staystitch

outer edge of pocket to front pants. Staystitch around clipped corner, Point A (see Fig.1).

▶3 Make up centre front inset by placing both pieces right sides together and stitching around both short ends and along one long side only. Trim corners, turn and press. Set centre front inset flat against centre front so that edges cover staystitching at Points A, and overlap raw edges by 1cm. Pin, then edgestitch around all three sides. Staystitch across top waist opening to hold in place.

▶4 Join front to back pants at sideseams. Stitch from top to bottom, then neaten seam allowances separately and press open. Repeat operation for inside leg seamlines.

▶5 To attach waistband, follow instructions exactly as for Skirt, Step 7.

▶6 Make buttonhole and attach button on waistband as marked on your pattern.

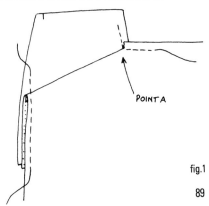

POINT A

fig.1

Streets Ahead
J A C K E T

YOU WILL NEED
2.10m of 115cm wide fabric
1 pair shoulder pads
8 buttons

This boxy, easy-to-sew collarless jacket is double-breasted, with patch pockets at the hipline to match those on the blouse. Designed to be worn with the pants or skirt, or over the dress or blouse, the effect of a mock collar could be achieved very easily by using a matching fabric.

▶1   Make darts in back bodice of jacket, stitch and press towards neckline. Make darts in two front bodice pieces, stitch and press downwards.

▶2   Make up and attach pockets exactly as for Blouse, Step 7.

▶3   Attach front bodice pieces to back bodice, at side seams and at shoulder lines, right sides together; stitch. Neaten all seam allowances separately and press open.

▶4   Attach back neck facing to two front facing pieces, right sides together; stitch. Press seam allowances open.

▶5   Set back neck facing against back neck, right sides together, and working around neckline to self-facing fold-backs at front, as notched. Baste, then stitch all round. Clip curves and turn

neckline so that right sides of facing and jacket are uppermost, then edgestitch around facing close to first line of stitching, machining about 6cm from each front folded edge. Neaten inner facing edge from hem, working up and around neckline to finish at hem; turn and press.

▶6   To finish hemline, fold back front facings as notched on your pattern, right sides together; stitch across hemline on each side of front jacket. Press front opening foldlines into place. Neaten remaining hem edge and turn up to wrong side around hemline as marked on your pattern. Pin, then slipstitch into place by hand.

▶7   To make up sleeves, join back arm seamlines, right sides together, and stitch from top to bottom. Neaten seam allowances separately and press open. Run a line of basting from back arm seamline to about 8cm beyond each sleevehead notch. Easing sleevehead around shoulderline, set left sleeve into left armhole, matching underarm notch to side seam, and sleevehead notch to shoulderline. Baste, then stitch all round. Trim seam allowances to 1cm, neaten together, then press away from neckline. Repeat for right sleeve. Finish cuffs by neatening raw edges and turning up to wrong side as notched. Slipstitch all round by hand; press.

▶8   Make buttonholes and attach buttons as marked on your pattern.

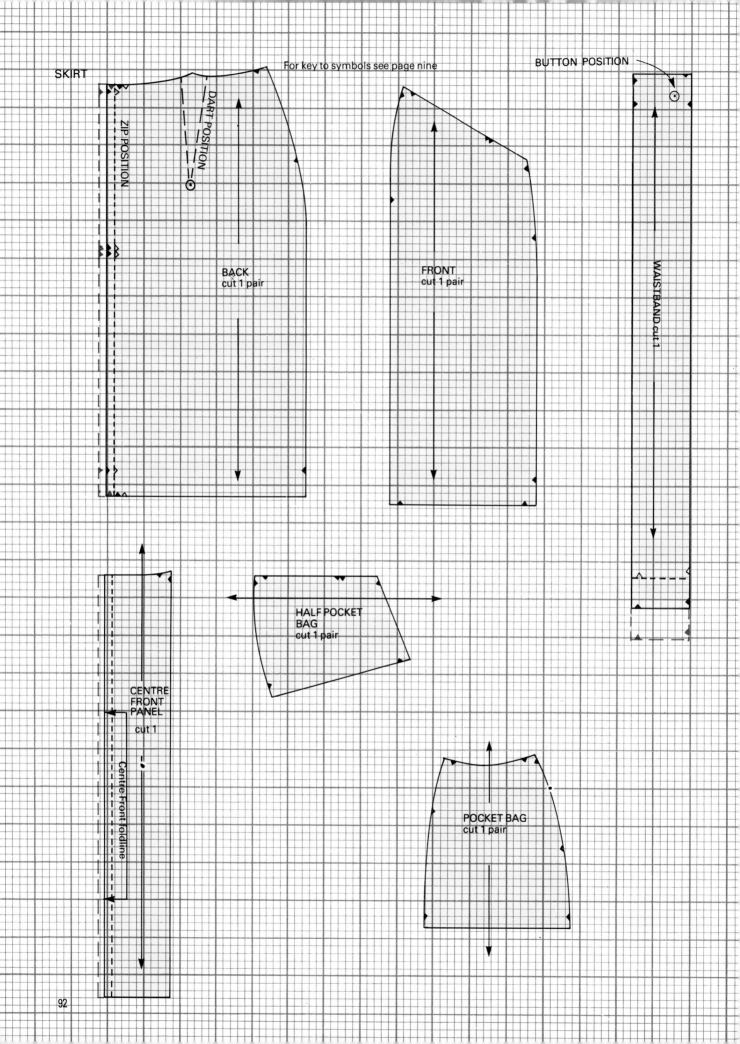

SKIRT

For key to symbols see page nine

BUTTON POSITION

ZIP POSITION

DART POSITION

BACK
cut 1 pair

FRONT
cut 1 pair

WAISTBAND cut 1

HALF POCKET
BAG
cut 1 pair

CENTRE
FRONT
PANEL
cut 1

Centre Front foldline

POCKET BAG
cut 1 pair

92

PANTS

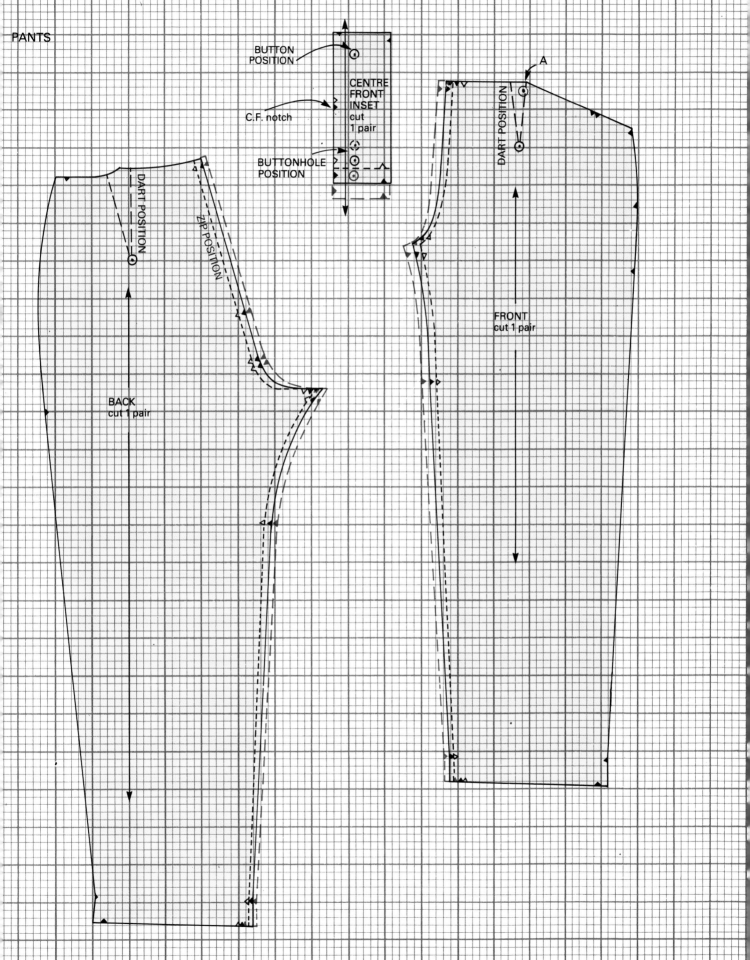

BUTTON
POSITION

CENTRE
FRONT
INSET
cut
1 pair

C.F. notch

BUTTONHOLE
POSITION

A

DART POSITION

FRONT
cut 1 pair

DART POSITION

ZIP POSITION

BACK
cut 1 pair

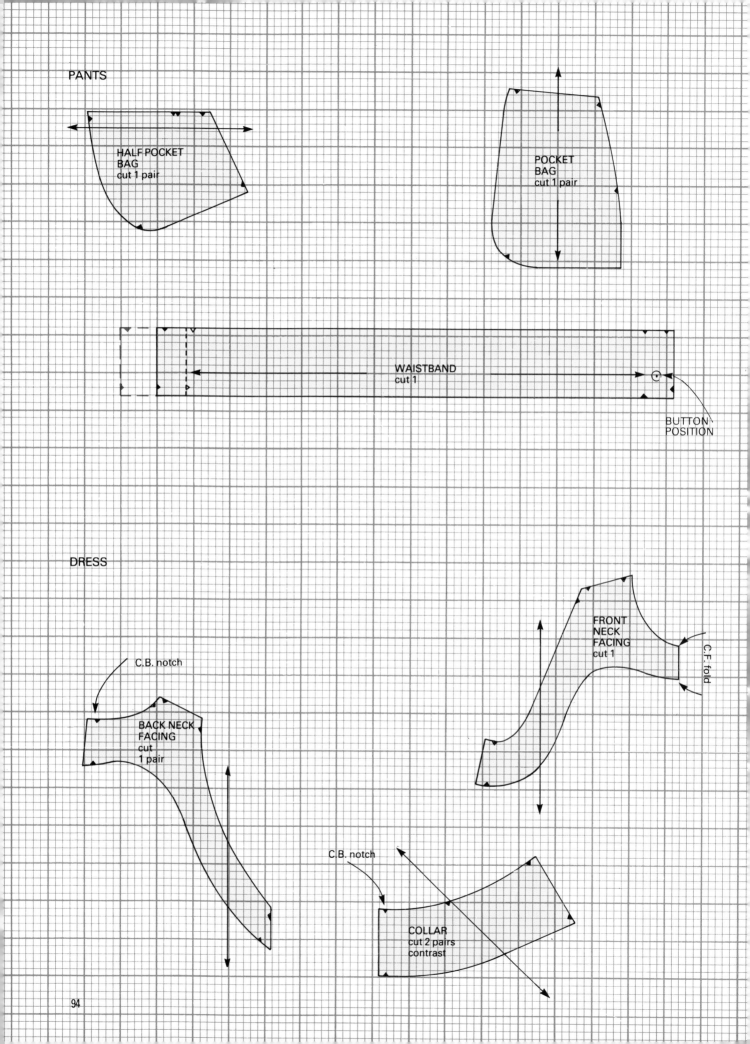

PANTS

HALF POCKET
BAG
cut 1 pair

POCKET
BAG
cut 1 pair

WAISTBAND
cut 1

BUTTON
POSITION

DRESS

C.B. notch

BACK NECK
FACING
cut
1 pair

FRONT
NECK
FACING
cut 1

C.F. fold

C.B. notch

COLLAR
cut 2 pairs
contrast

94

DRESS

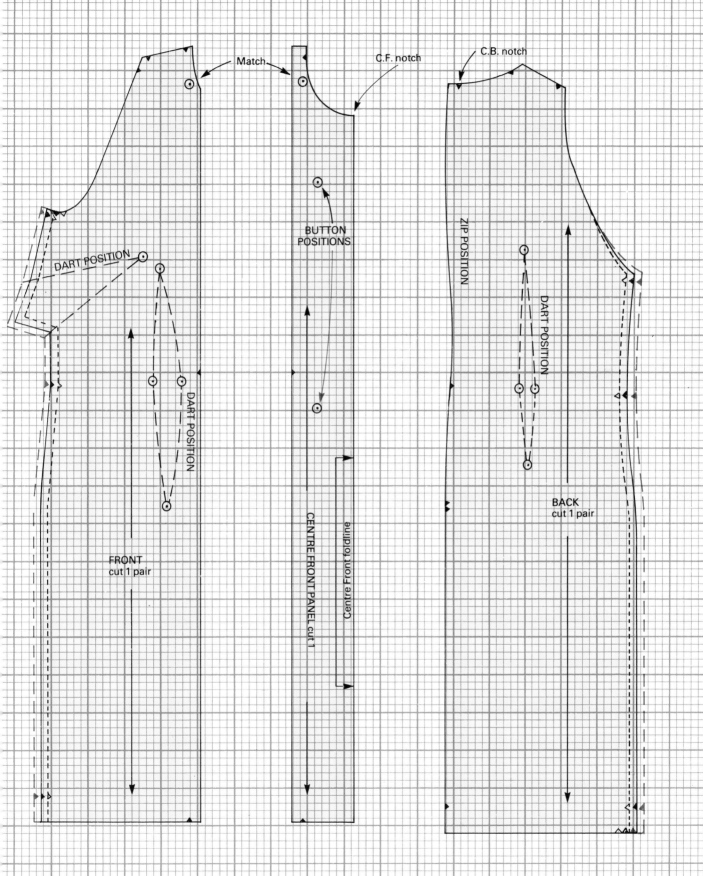

Match

C.F. notch

C.B. notch

BUTTON
POSITIONS

ZIP POSITION

DART POSITION

DART POSITION

DART POSITION

DART POSITION

CENTRE FRONT PANEL cut 1

Centre Front foldline

FRONT
cut 1 pair

BACK
cut 1 pair

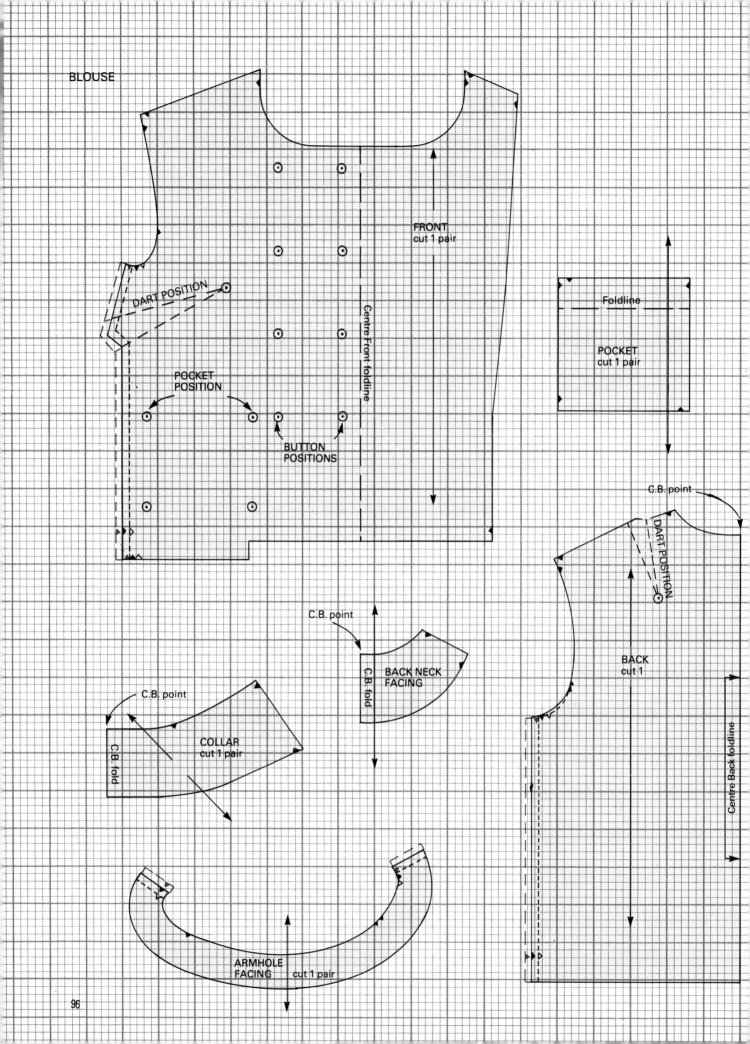

BLOUSE

FRONT
cut 1 pair

Centre Front foldline

DART POSITION

POCKET
POSITION

BUTTON
POSITIONS

Foldline

POCKET
cut 1 pair

C.B. point

DART POSITION

BACK
cut 1

Centre Back foldline

C.B. point

C.B. fold

BACK NECK
FACING

C.B. point

C.B. fold

COLLAR
cut 1 pair

ARMHOLE
FACING   cut 1 pair

96

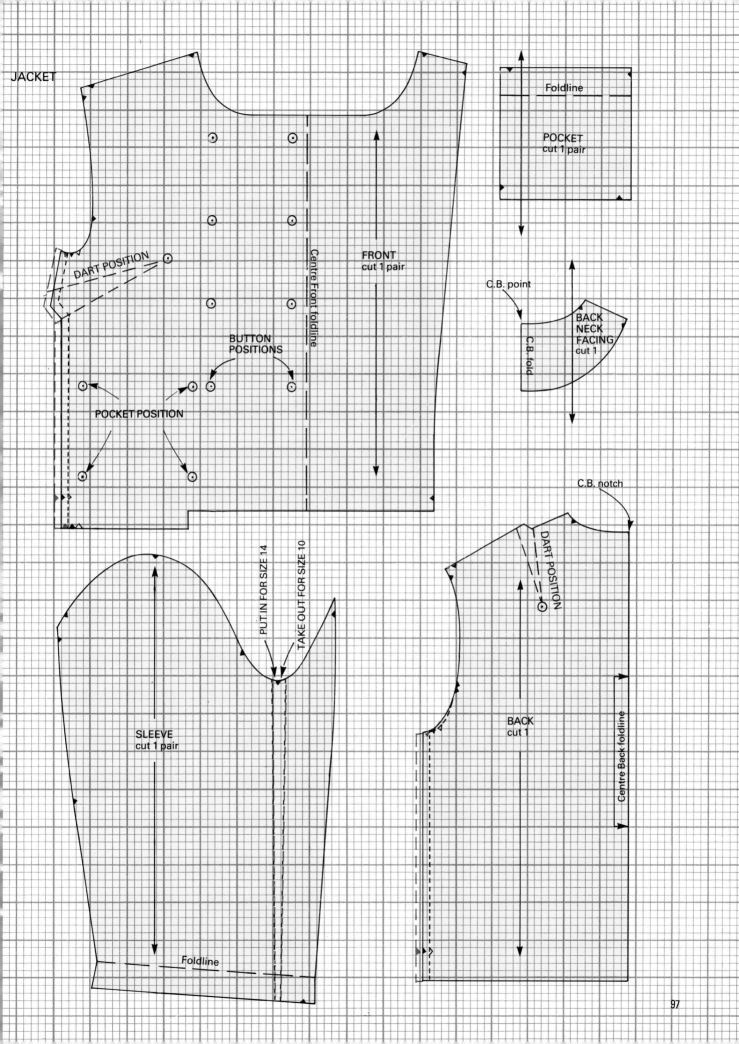

JACKET

POCKET
cut 1 pair

Foldline

C.B. point

C.B. fold

BACK
NECK
FACING
cut 1

DART POSITION

Centre Front foldline

FRONT
cut 1 pair

BUTTON
POSITIONS

POCKET POSITION

C.B. notch

DART POSITION

BACK
cut 1

Centre Back foldline

PUT IN FOR SIZE 14

TAKE OUT FOR SIZE 10

SLEEVE
cut 1 pair

Foldline

The original idea for this group of clothes was to design a capsule collection of summer season holiday separates which would relegate packing and carrying to a minimum. Bearing in mind hot, sparsely-clad beaches, it begins with a tie-fronted bikini, and then, working outwards, adds a front-buttoned skirt, side-buttoned shorts and a loose overshirt. These all carry the same tie detail and use of contrast fabrics. There is also a quick-to-sew sarong for an instant cover up after swimming or sitting in too much sun. All these designs – sarong apart – would look equally good made up in white or cream-coloured cotton or linen for everyday wear. Alternatively, simply ring the changes with plain and patterned fabrics. Try a range of pastels; or imagine tropical florals or bold geometrics over a single colour bikini!

HolidaySnaps

Holiday Snaps
B I K I N I

This simple bikini has very straightforward briefs bound in contrast fabric through which elastic is threaded, and a slightly more substantial bra, which is pleated at the sides to add shape to generous cups. The bra ties at centre front and is therefore constantly adjustable, and a detachable neck strap assures more support while swimming, thus solving the problem of strap marks and ensuring an even tan.

YOU WILL NEED

1.40m of 112cm wide fabric (main)
(or 1.40m of 95cm wide fabric (main))
40cm of 112cm wide fabric (contrast)
(or 40cm of 95cm wide fabric (contrast))
2 small buttons

(Note: cut 2 crossgrain strips of contrast binding, measuring 60cm by 3.5cm, for leg openings, and one crossgrain strip of contrast binding, 100cm long (for hips))

Briefs

▶1 To make up briefs, set right sides of front and back briefs together at crutch points. Stitch across each seamline and press seam allowances open. Set top briefs against lining, wrong sides together and matching front and back; stay-stitch all around to hold. Press.

▶2 Noting that from hereon, briefs and lining are made up as one, bind leg openings by placing binding against hip end of leg opening, right side to lining; stitch round to front hip end, machining 5mm in from raw edges. Press binding and seam allowance of briefs outwards, then press 5mm on remaining raw edge of binding to wrong side. Fold binding over to outside of briefs, wrapping fold just over the first line of stitching and pin. On right side of briefs, edgestitch binding in place all the way round leg opening; repeat for other leg and then press. Measure length of leg opening from back raw hip edge to front raw hip edge, then cut two pieces of elastic to this length. Thread one through each leg binding using a bodkin, stitching firmly across back to hold one end of elastic in place. At front hip, pull elastic through binding by an extra 8cm so that binding is slightly gathered, but not too tight; secure at front and trim away remaining elastic. Repeat for other side.

fig.1

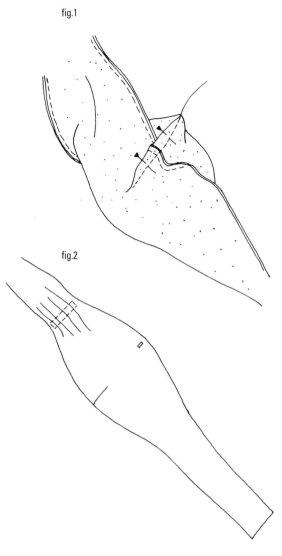

fig.2

▶3   Mark the centre point of your 100cm strip of binding, then match to centre front of front briefs lining, right sides together as before. Pin each side of binding flat to finish at outside edge of each leg opening, then stitch across front briefs. Press binding and seam allowances up towards waist. Join short ends of binding, right sides together, being careful not to twist them; press their seam allowances open. Attach join of binding to centre back briefs and stitch as before. Press under 5mm all around top raw edge of hip binding to wrong side, and repeat for lower edges of binding where they are separate from briefs. Now fold over pressed binding edge to set slightly over original stitching line on front and back briefs; pin in place. Where binding is separate from briefs, pin so that folded edges come together. Then on right side of briefs, edgestitch all around pinned folded edge of binding, leaving 1.5cm open at edge of back briefs through which to thread elastic.

▶4   Cut a length of elastic to fit your hips comfortably, thread through as before and secure with a small overlap. Close gap left in topstitching with a few topstitches and press completed briefs.

Bra

▶1   Bag out complete top by placing right sides together and pinning all round. Stitch all round, 1cm in from raw edges as marked, but leaving a 10cm gap at centre back through which to turn to right side.

▶2   Make bust darts as marked on your pattern

by opening out bust area of bra and folding so that dart line lies along the top of each fold. Pin dart into position, pinning from nothing at each bust point to 1.5cm deep at seamline (see Fig.1), then stitch across. Repeat for other dart.

▶3   Trim corners of bra strip, turn to right side and press carefully. Close gap by hand with slipstitches.

▶4   Mark sideseam positions from your pattern with pins placed at top and bottom of bra strip. Then make four small pleats facing downwards towards waist, so that finished width of sideseam measures 8cm. On right side of bra and working 5mm away from first stitching line, topstitch from top to bottom, pivot needle, stitch across bottom edge for 5mm, pivot needle again and topstitch up to top. Now pivot needle once more and stitch across top to finish at starting point (see Fig.2). Repeat for other side of bra.

▶5   Make a buttonhole at each top edge of bra cup as marked on your pattern. (Fig.2 also shows position.)

▶6   Make up neck strap by folding in each long raw edge of neck strap to wrong side by 5mm and pressing into position. Fold two pressed edges together, wrong sides together, and edgestitch down length of strap. Press, turn under or neaten ends, then attach a button 3cm from one end of strap. Button through buttonhole and attach other button to other end of strap so that it fits comfortably around neck and provides required bust support.

Holiday Snaps
SKIRT

YOU WILL NEED

For longer length, 1.45m of 112cm wide fabric (main) (or 1.45m of 95cm wide fabric (main))
For shorter length, 1.20m of 112cm wide fabric (main) (or 1.20m of 95cm wide fabric (main))
For both lengths, 70cm of 112cm wide fabric (contrast) (or 70cm of 95cm wide fabric (contrast))
5 small buttons

The pattern for the skirt shown here comes in two lengths, mini and above-the-knee, but is easily lengthened. It has unpressed pleats at the front and back for easy movement, inset side pockets and front button opening. The contrast ties at the waistband complete the casual, easy-to-wear look.

▶1   Attach a pocket bag to each front skirt piece at pocket opening, right sides together. Stitch, press bag and seam allowances away from skirt, then on right side of each pocket bag, edgestitch from top to bottom, through seam

allowances and close to original stitching line. Press each bag into position behind front skirt pieces, then on right side, edgestitch and top-stitch down each pocket opening, 5mm in from edge, as shown in Fig.1. Press.

▶2   Fold back 1cm at each front opening of skirt to wrong side and stitch from top to bottom. Then fold back each self facing at front skirt openings to right side, right sides together and so that centre front notches match; stitch across top from centre front to folded edge. Clip centre front seam allowance points to stitching line, turn and press. (See Fig.2.)

▶3   Set pleats on each front skirt piece as shown on your pattern and staystitch into position. Now attach a pocket piece to each

fig.1

fig.2

pocket bag, right sides together and matching notches; stitch around inner curved edge of each pocket. Neaten seam allowances together and set each pocket flat behind pleats at waistline; pin into position at waistline and at sideseams.

▶4   Set pleats on back skirt as shown on your pattern and staystitch into position.

▶5   Join sideseams, right sides together, and stitch from top to bottom. Neaten seam allowances together, then press each seam allowance towards back skirt. Working on right side, edgestitch and topstitch from top to bottom, 5mm in from edge and through seam allowances.

▶6   Fold waistband tie in half lengthways, right sides together and make ties by stitching from centre front notch to each corner and across end of each tie. Trim corners, turn and press, clipping into seamline at each centre front point on tie. Attach one side of waistband to waistline of skirt, right sides together and matching centre front and centre back points; stitch from centre front to centre front, all the way round waistline.

Turn under remaining raw edge of inside waistband by 1cm, lay foldline just over the top of first line of stitching, then pin all round. On right side, edgestitch round waistband tie from centre front to centre front points and through to wrong side, catching inside waistband as pinned. Strengthen clipped stitching line at each centre front point if necessary with a few handstitches and press.

▶7   To finish hem, fold front facing back onto skirt front, right sides together, and matching centre front notches at hemline. Stitch across facing at hemline, 1.5cm up from raw edge. Turn to right side and then, folding under 5mm at raw hemline edge, stitch all round. Turn under 1cm again to wrong side and edgestitch around inner folded edge of hem through to right side. Press.

▶8   Press facing at centre front openings into position from top to bottom of skirt, against the wrong side, then make buttonholes and attach buttons as marked on your pattern.

Holiday Snaps
S H O R T S

YOU WILL NEED
1.25m of 112cm wide fabric (main)
(or 1.25m of 95cm wide fabric (main))
70cm of 112cm wide fabric (contrast)
(or 70cm of 95cm wide fabric (contrast))
4 small buttons

These brief shorts, which could be cut longer if preferred, have inset side pockets, unpressed pleats on the front and back and a contrast waistband tie. They are side-buttoning.

▶1   Join centre front seam of shorts, right sides together, and stitch from top to bottom. Neaten seam allowances together and press towards right side. Edgestitch and topstitch 5mm in from edge, machining down right front shorts from top to bottom and through seam allowances. Repeat operation for back shorts, pressing seam allowances towards left side and edgestitching and topstitching down left back shorts. On inside of shorts, clip seam allowances at crutch curve to topstitching line to ease.

▶2   Attach pocket bags to each front pocket line, right sides together; stitch from top to bottom on right shorts and from top to bottom and around corner to side seam on left shorts as indicated in Fig.1. Clip seam allowances at point marked A on the pattern on left front shorts so that they will fold back to wrong side with ease, then press seam allowances and pocket bags outwards, away from shorts. Now edgestitch

down pocket bag, close to first line of stitching; work from top to bottom on right side and around corner to side seam on left side, stitching through seam allowances. Press pocket bags to inside, flat against front shorts, and edgestitch and topstitch 5mm in from edge, as shown in Fig.1.

▶3   Set pocket pieces behind each pocket bag, pinning and stitching around inside curve of each pocket. Neaten seam allowances together and press. Set pleats on front and back shorts as marked on your pattern, and staystitch to hold in place. Then on front shorts, set and pin pocket pieces flat behind pleats at waistline and at sideseams; staystitch to secure.

▶4   Set front shorts against back shorts, right sides together, and stitch from top to bottom of right sideseam only. Neaten seam allowances together and press towards back. On right side, edgestitch and topstitch 5mm in from edge on right back shorts, machining from top to bottom and through seam allowances.

▶5   On left sideseam opening, turn back 1cm on raw edge of front shorts to wrong side and stitch from top to bottom. Turn back self facing to right side, so that right sides come together and sideseam notches match; stitch from

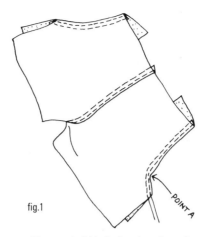

fig.1

sideseam to folded edge, 1cm down from top raw edge. Clip seam allowances at waist sideseam point to stitching line, then turn to right side. Fold facing back on itself at hemline, right sides together and matching sideseam notches, then stitch across facing at hemline, 1.5cm up from raw hem edge. Turn to right side and press front

opening from top to bottom. Repeat for back left opening of shorts.

▶6   Place right sides of shorts together at under-crutch point; stitch from back to front hem and around crutch. Trim seam allowances to 1cm, neaten together, press towards back shorts and then on right side, edgestitch and topstitch 5mm in from edge, machining from hem to hem.

▶7   Follow Step 6 of Skirt pattern for waist-band tie instructions, beginning and ending at left sideseam opening instead of at centre front, as with skirt.

▶8   To finish hems, turn up 5mm to wrong side and stitch all round. Turn up 1cm again and on wrong side, edgestitch around inner folded edge of leg, through to right side. Repeat for other leg and press.

▶9   Make buttonholes and attach buttons as marked on your pattern.

Holiday Snaps
V E S T

This sportily styled little top has cut away armhole openings and front pleat interest. The contrast binding is finished with two small buttons at the left shoulder opening.

YOU WILL NEED

1.40m of 112cm wide fabric (main)
(or 1.40m of 95cm wide fabric (main))
50cm of 112cm wide fabric, inclusive of bindings (contrast)
(or 50cm of 95cm wide fabric, inclusive of bindings (contrast))
2 small buttons

(Note: also cut 3 crossgrain strips of contrast binding, measuring 70cm by 3.5cm, for neck and armhole bindings.)

▶1   Match front and back seamlines, right sides together, and stitch from top to bottom. Neaten seam allowances together and press front seam allowance towards right side and back seam allowance towards left side. On right side of vest, edgestitch and topstitch 5mm in from edge, down both centre front and centre back seams and through seam allowances. Press.

▶2   At right shoulder only, set right sides of front and back shoulder seams together. Stitch, neaten seam allowances together and press towards back. On right side, edgestitch and topstitch 5mm in from edge, through seam allowances. Press. Leave left shoulder open at this stage.

▶3   Make pleats on front neckline as marked on your pattern and staystitch into position. (See Fig.1.)

▶4   Attach binding around neck, setting right

sides together and beginning and ending at raw shoulder edge. Stitch 5mm in from raw edges all round, then press binding and seam allowances outwards, away from bodice. Turn binding to inside, turning under 5mm at remaining raw edge so that it just covers the first line of stitching; pin all round. On right side of binding, edgestitch close to join between binding and bodice, all the way round, catching inner folded and pinned edge on wrong side of binding. Press and repeat this operation on left armhole opening. For closed right armhole, attach and finish binding exactly as before, but fold under 5mm of binding at shoulderline starting point as shown in Fig.2, and finish by overlapping end of binding across starting point.

▶5   To finish off opening at left shoulder, lay a strip of binding the same width as before across each short raw shoulder edge, turning in ends at each end of binding (illustrated in Fig.3); bind exactly as above. Secure each end with a handstitch or two if necessary and press. Make two buttonholes and attach tiny buttons to correspond (Fig.3).

▶6   To finish hem, turn under 5mm to wrong side at hem and stitch all round. Turn under 1cm again and then, working from wrong side through to right side, edgestitch around inner folded hem edge. Press.

fig.2

fig.3

fig.1

Holiday Snaps
S H I R T

YOU WILL NEED

2.55mm of 112cm wide fabric (main)
(or 2.55m of 95cm wide fabric (main))
1m of 112cm wide fabric, inclusive of bindings (contrast)
(or 1.30m of 95cm wide fabric, inclusive of bindings (contrast))

(Note: also cut 2 crossgrain strips of contrast binding, measuring 60cm by 6cm, for cuffs.)

Loosely cut and casual, this easy-to-wear overshirt would look equally good worn as a dress, cut long or short. It is front buttoning, with roomy sleeves which can be rolled back, and an easy-to-make collar which extends into ties. Three patch pockets are bound with contrast fabric to match the contrast collar and rever, and the cuffs.

▶1 Join shirt back to two front shirt sections at shoulderlines, right sides together, and stitch. Neaten seam allowances together and press towards back. On right side of back shirt, edgestitch and topstitch each shoulder seam 5mm in from edge and through seam allowances. Press.

▶2 Join right sides of sideseams together and stitch from underarm notch to hem, on each side. Finish exactly as in Step 1, pivoting needle at each underarm point and stitching horizontally across back and seam allowances for 5mm, and returning to hem with topstitching line 5mm in from edge, as before.

▶3 To make up sleeves, join each sleeve along underarm seamline, right sides together, and stitch from underarm edge to cuff edge. Neaten seam allowances together, pressing towards back on each sleeve and then on right side, edgestitch and topstitch 5mm in from edge as before, machining from cuff edge to underarm edge. Press. Set cuff binding against cuff edge of sleeves, right sides together and matching raw edges. Beginning at underarm seamline, fold cuff binding as in Fig.2 of Vest to neaten, then stitch round; press seam allowances and binding away from sleeve. Next fold 1cm at remaining raw edge of binding to wrong side and, setting foldline directly over first line of stitching, pin all round. Turning to right side, edgestitch binding in place all round, close to first line of stitching and through inside binding edge. Repeat for other cuff and press. Set in each sleeve, right sides together, remembering to direct each underarm seam allowance towards shirt back. Stitch all round, then neaten seam allowances together and press towards neckline, clipping each seam allowance at underarm point to ease. On right side, edgestitch and topstitch 5mm in from edge, machining from underarm point to underarm point; pivot needle and stitch horizontally across for 5mm at underarm points to make connection between edgestitching and top-stitching.

▶4 Make up collar and rever as follows: you will be forming a four-cornered star shape with each join of collar to rever. Firstly, place two collar pieces right sides together and stitch along long curved outer edge and down each side to point marked A. Trim each sharp outer point of collar (see Fig.1). To set roll on undercollar, edgestitch close to original stitching line along long outer curved edge of undercollar, through seam allowances, to within about 5cm of each

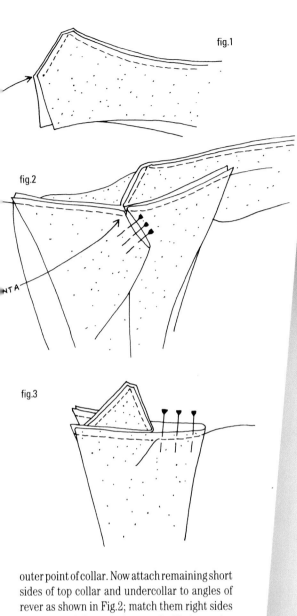

fig.1

fig.2

fig.3

outer point of collar. Now attach remaining short
sides of top collar and undercollar to angles of
rever as shown in Fig.2; match them right sides
together and then stitch on each side into point
A. Lastly, stitch across remaining open fold of
rever to close, as shown in Fig.3. Press open two
seam allowances joining collar to rever, then
turn collar to right side and on each side press
carefully to bottom of rever at Point B. Repeat
whole operation for other rever.

▶5   Attach undercollar and under-rever to
neck opening of shirt, right sides together;
match notches at points B and at shoulderlines.
Pin, then stitch all round. At centre front
self-facings, neaten long raw opening edges by
turning in 5mm to wrong side and stitching from
point B to hemline on each side. Fold back facing
onto shirt front at fold notch, right sides
together, and on each side stitch from outer fold
across to point B only. Slash into point B through
seam allowance to allow you to turn to right side
and set facing flat behind shirt front. Press.

▶6   Bag out each tie by first folding in half
lengthways, right sides together, and then stitch-

ing from point B down to bottom of tie and across to finish at foldline. Trim corners, turn and press each tie.

▶7   Lay shirt on ironing board so that top collar and revers face uppermost and lie flat. Press shirt, collar and rever seam allowances towards collar and rever. On each side, clip curves around neckline to ease and slash into shirt front seam allowance at point B to allow it to fold towards rever. Then, turning under 1cm on remaining raw edges of collar and each rever, set foldline directly over original stitching line and pin into position from point B to B; work all around neckline, enclosing seam allowances. Next either slipstitch by hand to secure, or turning shirt so that right sides are uppermost, edgestitch from point B, machining up and around under-rever and collar to finish at same Point B on other side, and stitching through folded inner collar and rever edge as set. (See Fig.4.). Press.

▶8   At hem, turn back front facings as notched, right sides together, and stitch across facings to secure. Turn facings to right side and, working from top to bottom, press flat against shirt front openings. Neaten top of facing at points B by turning under and catching with a few hand-stitches. To finish hemline, turn up 5mm to wrong side and stitch all around hem. Turn up 1cm again, and on wrong side, edgestitch all the way round hem and through to right side, machining close to inner folded edge. Press.

fig.4

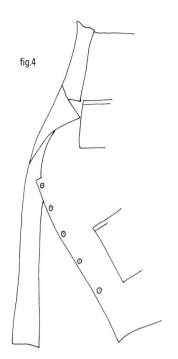

▶9   To make pockets, set binding against pocket, right sides together and matching top raw edges. Stitch across, 1cm down from top raw edge. Press seam allowances and binding to-wards top of pocket, and then press under 1cm at top raw edge of binding to wrong side. Fold binding back on itself so that right sides are together, then matching folded edge of binding to stitching line, stitch across sides, 1cm in from each edge. Trim and turn to right side. Press, then neaten remaining raw edges of pocket. Pin inside of binding directly over top of first stitch-ing line, then on right side, edgestitch across bottom of binding and through inside of binding as pinned. Press remaining neatened edges of pocket to wrong side by 1 cm, then set and pin against front shirt as marked on your pattern. Edgestitch 1cm in from top opening corner down and around pocket. Finish as you began. (See Fig.5.) Press.

▶10   Make buttonholes and attach buttons as marked on your pattern.

fig.5

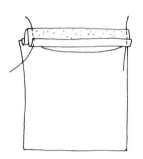

YOU WILL NEED
2.50m of 115cm wide fabric (or 2.50cm of 95cm wide fabric)

Holiday Snaps
S A R O N G

Simply turn 5mm on each raw edge to wrong side and stitch all round. Turn under 1cm again to wrong side and stitch all round. Press.

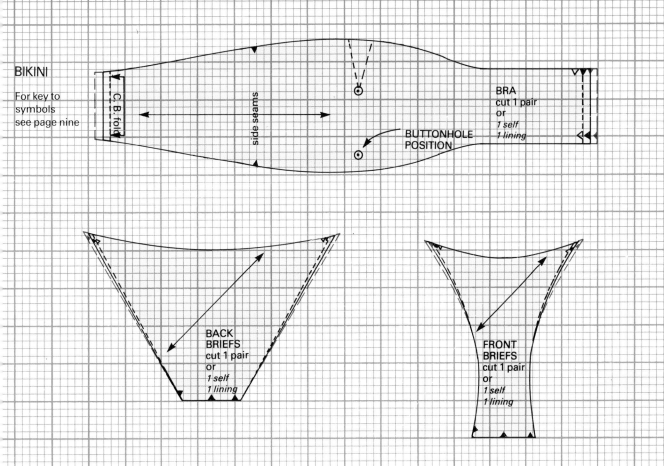

BIKINI

For key to symbols see page nine

C. B. fold

side seams

BUTTONHOLE POSITION

BRA
cut 1 pair
or
1 self
1 lining

BACK
BRIEFS
cut 1 pair
or
1 self
1 lining

FRONT
BRIEFS
cut 1 pair
or
1 self
1 lining

TOP

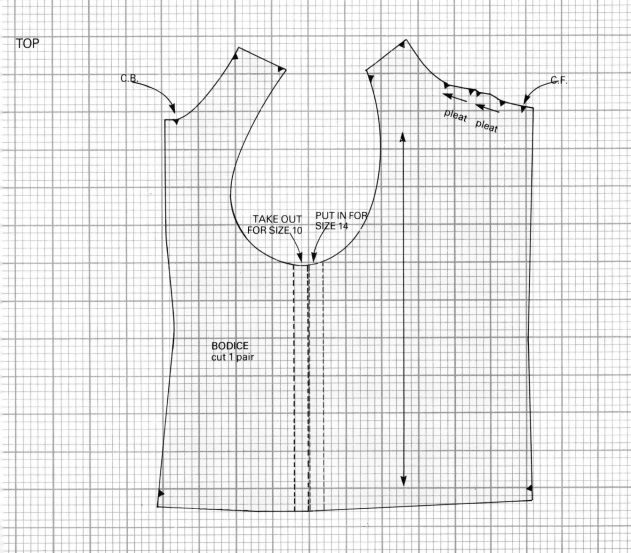

C.B.

C.F.

pleat   *pleat*

TAKE OUT
FOR SIZE 10

PUT IN FOR
SIZE 14

BODICE
cut 1 pair

SHORTS

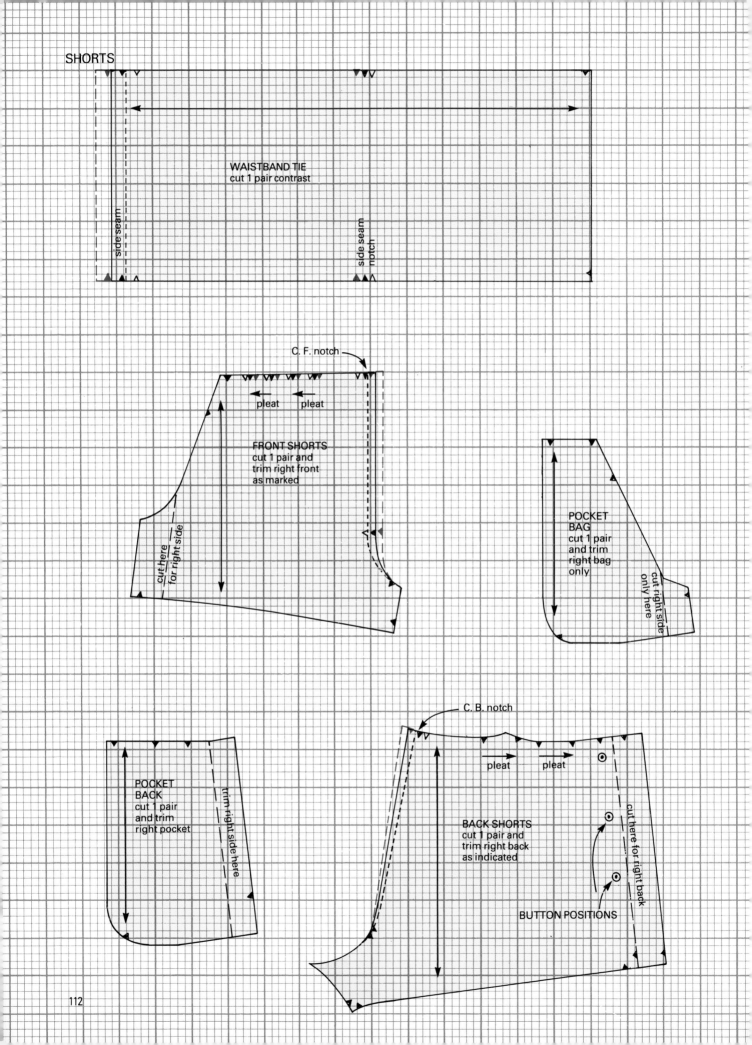

WAISTBAND TIE
cut 1 pair contrast

side seam

side seam
notch

C. F. notch

pleat   pleat

FRONT SHORTS
cut 1 pair and
trim right front
as marked

cut here
for right side

POCKET
BAG
cut 1 pair
and trim
right bag
only

cut right side
only here

POCKET
BACK
cut 1 pair
and trim
right pocket

trim right side here

C. B. notch

pleat   pleat

BACK SHORTS
cut 1 pair and
trim right back
as indicated

cut here for right back

BUTTON POSITIONS

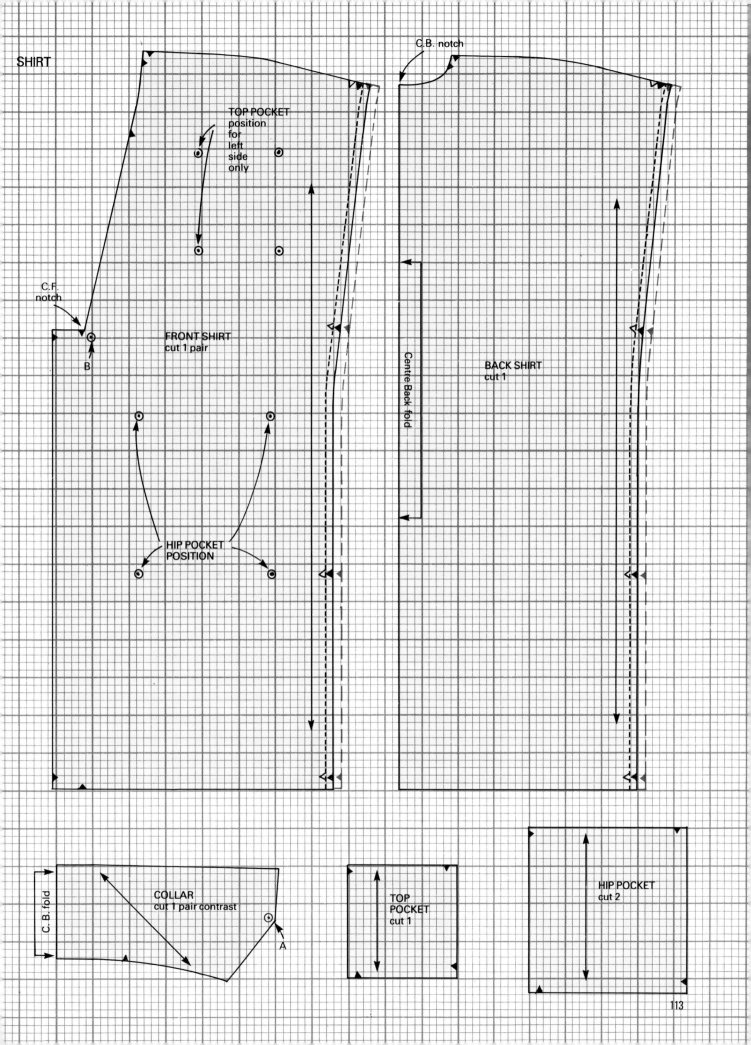

SHIRT

TOP POCKET
position
for
left
side
only

C.B. notch

C.F.
notch

B

FRONT SHIRT
cut 1 pair

BACK SHIRT
cut 1

Centre Back fold

HIP POCKET
POSITION

COLLAR
cut 1 pair contrast

C. B. fold

A

TOP
POCKET
cut 1

HIP POCKET
cut 2

113

SHIRT

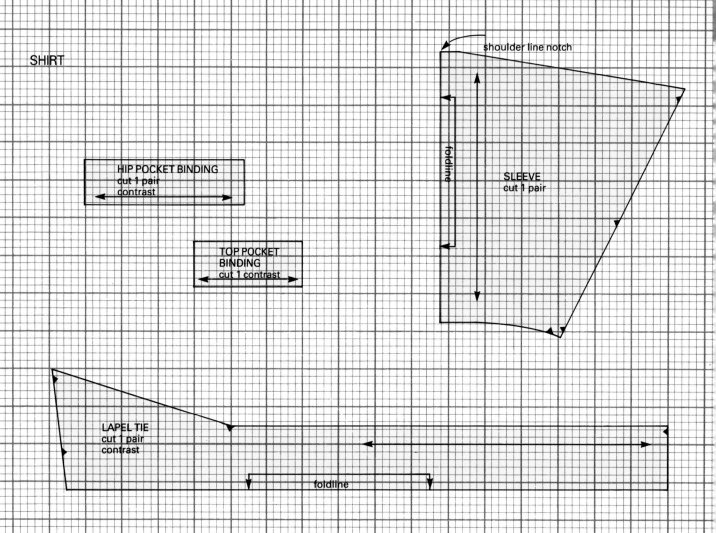

HIP POCKET BINDING
cut 1 pair
contrast

TOP POCKET
BINDING
cut 1 contrast

SLEEVE
cut 1 pair

shoulder line notch

foldline

LAPEL TIE
cut 1 pair
contrast

foldline

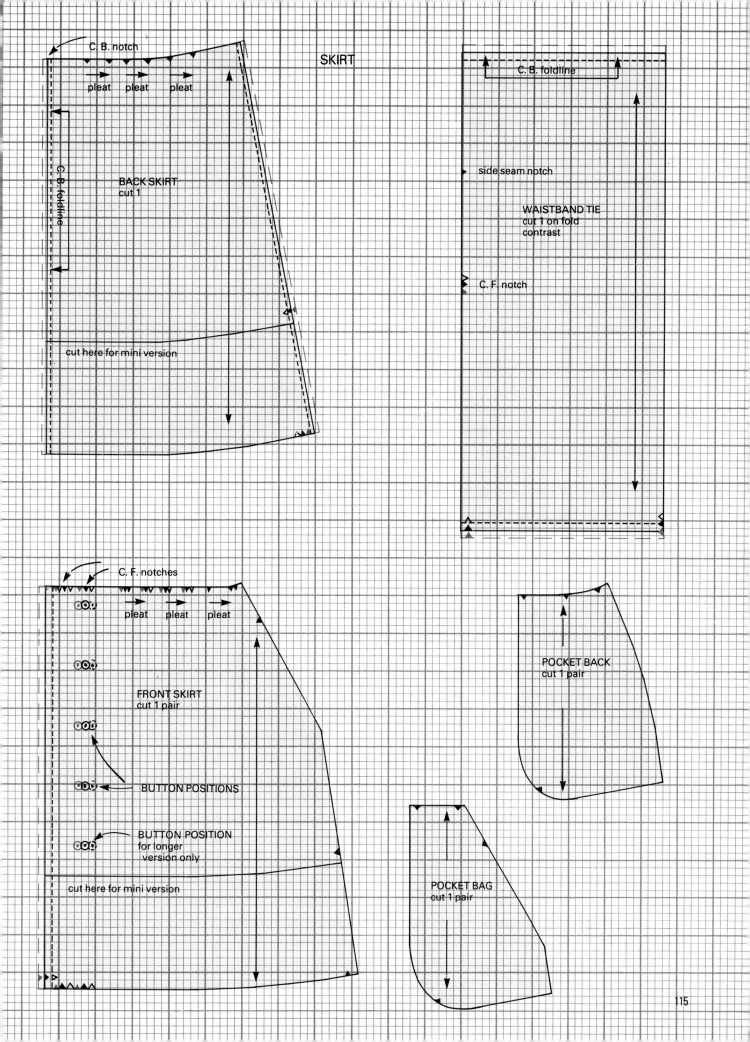

SKIRT

C. B. notch

pleat   pleat   pleat

C. B. foldline

BACK SKIRT
cut 1

cut here for mini version

C. B. foldline

WAISTBAND TIE
cut 1 on fold
contrast

side seam notch

C. F. notch

C. F. notches

pleat   pleat   pleat

FRONT SKIRT
cut 1 pair

BUTTON POSITIONS

BUTTON POSITION
for longer
version only

cut here for mini version

POCKET BACK
cut 1 pair

POCKET BAG
cut 1 pair

115

The aim in designing these silky evening clothes was to try for a simple unusual cut and focus as much interest on the back as possible. The fronts of the overshirt and coat have been deliberately left simple, the coat offering only a draped collar; the little vest is minimal – the sort of 'back and front' that costs a small fortune in the shops. The dress is particularly adventurous. Not only does it wrap around the back of the body to form a deeply contrasting back collar, but it can be knotted at the hip or waist, and will fall into a multitude of shapes. Making up all these garments in pure silk satin may seem a luxury, but they will repay their cost many times over. Duplicating one outfit in wool challis shows further exactly how versatile these designs can be. (For notes on working silk, refer back to page 8.)

After Dark

After Dark D R E S S

This spectacular wraparound evening dress has a deep 'V' front, a deeper wrapped 'V' back and contrast back collar. It can be knotted at the hip or around the waist.

▶1 Thread your machine with contrast coloured thread, then neaten inner long curved edge of both contrast lining pieces. Set each lining piece against each dress section at armholes, right sides together and matching curves; stitch all round taking a 5mm seam

allowance and pivoting needle at each sharp armhole corner. Stitch again around each sharp corner to strengthen, clip curves and into corners, and then turn linings to inside of dress pieces. Press carefully.

▶2 Pin two dress sections, right sides together, down centre front seamline, then pin and stitch contrast lining down same centre front seamline, right sides together; machine from centre front notch to lower neatened edge of facing.

Change thread to main dress colour, then stitch centre front seamline of dress from notch marking top of seamline to lower notch marking top of centre front split. Neaten seam allowances separately and press open.

▶3 Set lining into position at neck edge of dress, pinning loosely. Now turn this seamline inside out so that right sides come together, and pin carefully from centre front, up and around neck. (At this stage a tunnel will be formed which will fill with fabric as you work towards the

first right-angled edge of neckline. Don't worry about this; when stitched it will automatically turn back to the right side.) Continue pinning fabric around right angle and finish at far neatened edge of contrast facing. Stitch from this edge all around to centre front notch point as pinned. To strengthen, run another line of stitching 2mm outside first stitching line and along seam allowance, working from centre front point to notch, 20cm beyond armhole position. Trim right-angled seam allowance and pull fabric back through 'tunnel' to right side. Repeat for other side. Press carefully, pressing seam allowances open down centre front.

▶4 To finish remaining raw edges of dress, turn in 5mm to wrong side, beginning at centre front upper split point and continuing around hem to finish at back lining edge. Press. Turn under 1cm again to wrong side and stitch all the way round, close to inner folded edge and through to right side. Press, then turn to right side and edgestitch all round outer edge of dress. Press and repeat for other side of dress.

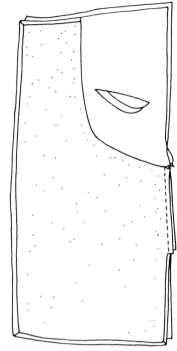

VIEW OF INSIDE OF DRESS, FOLDED IN HALF

After Dark
O V E R S H I R T

YOU WILL NEED
2.80m of 118cm wide fabric

This 'V' fronted overshirt features a split at its lower front seamline, and deep, roomy sleeves. The deeply 'V'd back bodice finishes in draped sections which can either be knotted or tied around the hips or left loose.

▶1 Make darts at shoulders, placing right sides together; stitch. Neaten seam allowances separately and press open; press closed part of dart seam allowance flat against shoulderline.

▶2 Set bodice pieces together at centre back, right sides together and matching notches; stitch from top to bottom. Neaten seam allowances separately and press open. Fold bodice so that underarm seamlines come right sides together and stitch from underarm point to cuff edge on each side. Neaten seam allowances separately and press open. Set aside.

▶3 Attach back neck facing to two front neck facing pieces at shoulderlines, right sides together; stitch. Press seam allowances open. Set against neck edge of shirt, right sides together, matching shoulder seamlines and notches. Pin, then stitch all round from open

centre front point around back neck to open centre front point. Turn so that facing and bodice are right sides uppermost. Now edgestitch around facing, close to first line of stitching and through seam allowances. Neaten inner raw edge of facing all round, then press facing to wrong side of neckline; to ease, clip seam allowance curves at back neck where necessary. Attach facing to inside of bodice at shoulderlines with a few handstitches.

▶4 To finish cuffs, turn 5mm in to wrong side; stitch all round. Turn in 1cm again to wrong side and edgestitch all round, close to inner folded edge and through to right side. On right side, edgestitch close to lower folded edge of cuff, pull threads to inside and tie off, threading away with a needle.

▶5 Join two lower shirt pieces at centre front, right sides together; stitch from top to centre front split point. Neaten seam allowances separately and press open. Now join bodice to lower shirt at centre front, right sides together; pin together around to underarm notch and seamline on each side. Stitch, then neaten seam allowances together. (See Fig.1.) Continue to attach back shirt section to back bodice, working around to match centre back seam to centre

back notches. Stitch across each side and then neaten seam allowances together.

▶6   To finish hemline, neaten by first turning 5mm under to wrong side and then stitching all round from centre front to centre back, on each side. Press, turn in 1cm again to wrong side and stitch through to right side; work all the way round, close to inner folded edge. Press, then on right side, edgestitch close to hem edge all the way round hemline, making a 'V' shape at centre front and and centre back split points as in Skirt, Fig.2. Press, then finish cuffs in exactly the same way. Press again, pulling all threads to the inside, tying off and threading away with a needle.

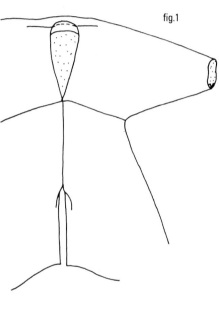

fig.1

After Dark
S K I R T

YOU WILL NEED
2.40cm of 118cm wide fabric
1 zip, 20cm long
2 pairs hooks and eyes

The skirt featured here has a hip basque that curves low to a deep point at centre back, with zip fastening. The skirt is attached to the hips by means of an increasingly deep fold of fabric which forms extra drape at the centre back. This drape can be worn floating, tied at the back, or it can be wrapped around the bottom and hips to form a knot at the front.

▶1   Set top and under-hip basques right sides together, matching notches; stitch around waistline only. Stitch again 2mm outside first stitching line to strengthen. Clip curves of seam allowance to second stitching line all around waistline, then turn so that right side of hip basque and its facing are uppermost. On facing, edgestitch all the way round, machining close to waistline edge and through seam allowances. Turn facing to inside and press carefully into position. Staystitch down length of centre back opening. Join centre back seams of hip basque, right sides together, and stitch from notch marking bottom of zip, to bottom of point. Baste

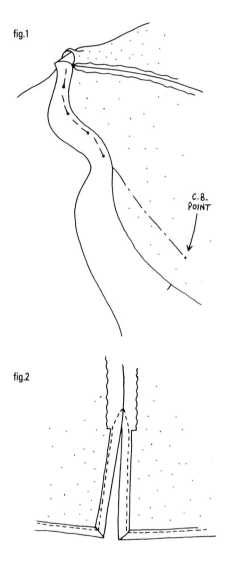

fig.1

C.B.
POINT

fig.2

remaining seamline to waist, neaten seam allowances separately and press open. Beginning 5mm down from waistline, attach by hand using stabstitch, tucking in raw top ends of zip behind seam allowances. Baste around lower hip edge of basque, 1cm in from raw edge, and set aside.

▶2   Join centre front of two skirt pieces, right sides together, and stitch from top notch marking skirt split. Neaten seam allowances separately and press open.

▶3   On both skirt pieces, run a line of basting to mark the long curved front and back hipline, as shown on your pattern. Now fold top edge of skirt back to wrong side, overlapping this line by 1cm so that wrong sides are together; work from centre back, around front, returning to centre back again. (See Fig.1.) Baste all round, 1cm away from raw folded inner edge.

▶4   Working with your hand inside hip basque, and starting at centre front point, set skirt flat behind hip basque, matching basting lines,

notches, and with raw edges together. Pin all round to centre back point – you may find it easier to work from the inside outwards. Repeat for other side. Next stitch all round from centre back to centre back point, 1cm in from raw edge, being careful to keep fold formed in skirt out of the way. Neaten seam allowances together all the way round; press carefully. Do not press hip fold since this is designed to drape naturally around the body when worn.

▶5   Neaten remaining raw edges of skirt, starting at centre back, by firstly turning in 5mm to wrong side and stitching all round to centre back point. Press carefully, then turn in 1cm again to wrong side and stitch all round; work close to inner folded edge, through to right side, making a small stitched 'V' at centre front as shown in Fig.2. Press, then on right side, edgestitch all round hemline to finish.

▶6   Attach two hooks and eyes, or handmade loops, to centre back skirt at waist. Press.

YOU WILL NEED

For sizes 10 and 12, 1m of 118cm wide fabric (includes enough for bindings)
For size 14, 1.30m of 118cm wide fabric (includes enough for bindings)

After Dark
V E S T

This very simple vest has no bust darts and is bound at the neck and armhole openings with strips of self-binding. It is topstitched to finish.

▶1   Set front to back vest at sideseams, right sides together; stitch from top to bottom. Neaten seam allowances separately and press open. Join shoulder seams in exactly the same way.

▶2   To bind neckline, follow instructions exactly as for Holiday Snaps Vest, Step 4. Finish armholes using same method.

▶3   Finish hemline exactly as for Holiday Snaps Vest, Step 6.

After Dark
C O A T

YOU WILL NEED

3.60m of 118cm wide fabric

Deeply cut sleeves and floating, draped panels form the design basis of this loose, easy-to-wear evening coat. The angled line of the bodice is further accentuated by the use of topstitching. A simple, draped collar, cut on the cross, completes the casual, relaxed look.

▶1 Make shoulderline darts on bodice pieces by placing right sides together and stitching from neck edge to bottom of dart as marked on your pattern. Neaten seam allowances separately and press open; allow the narrower part of each seam allowance, near its point, to lie evenly and flat on each side of seamline.

▶2 Attach two bodice pieces at centre back, right sides together; stitch from top to bottom. Neaten seam allowances separately and press open.

▶3 Join sleeves at underarm seams, right sides together; stitch from cuff edge to underarm point on each side. Neaten seam allowances separately and press open.

▶4 Attach right bodice to right lower coat, right sides together, matching centre back and front, and underarm seamline, to underarm notch. Stitch from centre front point, around to underarm point, leaving seam allowances clear. Stitch from underarm point to centre back. Neaten seam allowances together. Repeat for left side, then press seam allowances upwards towards neck.

▶5 Beginning at centre back, neaten all around back drape, hemline and front opening as follows: turn 5mm in to wrong side and stitch all round. Press, then turn in 1cm again to wrong side and stitch all round, close to inner folded edge and through to right side, forming a 'V' shape at centre back. Pull threads to inside and tie off. Press and then on right side, edgestitch all around outer folded edge of drape, hem and front opening. Repeat for other side and press.

▶6 Join collar pieces at centre back, right sides together and stitch, pressing seam allowances open. Lay one long collar side against neck opening, right sides together, matching raw edges and centre back and shoulderline notches, and overlapping centre front join point by 1cm. Stitch all round. To strengthen, repeat stitching 2mm outside first stitching line. Clip seam allowance at curves and press seam allowances and collar away from bodice. Turn back collar points at front, right sides together, so that raw edges match; stitch across. (See Fig.1.) Trim point and turn, then repeat for other side. Folding 1cm along remaining raw edge of collar to wrong side, set in position, matching notches, just over first line of stitching; tuck in seam allowances at centre front. On right side, stitch around neckline from centre front to centre front, machining directly through first line of stitching and at same time catching in inner folded edge all round; alternatively, slipstitch all round by hand. Press seamline only; do not press outer fold of collar, except at short ends.

▶7 Set centre back seam allowance at bottom to lie flat with a few handstitches, then on right side, edgestitch from centre front along bodice line, through seam allowances, to underarm point. Stitch a half 'V' to 5mm away from first line of stitching, and return with a topstitching line to centre front. Pull threads to inside and tie off, threading away from centre front with a needle. Repeat for other side of front bodice. Repeat stitching for back bodice, stitching a half 'V' shape at each underarm point.

▶8 Finish cuffs exactly as for Overshirt, Step 4.

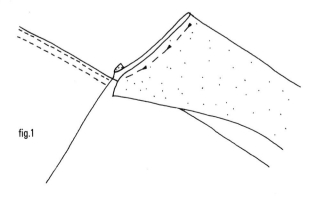

fig.1

DRESS

For key to symbols see page nine

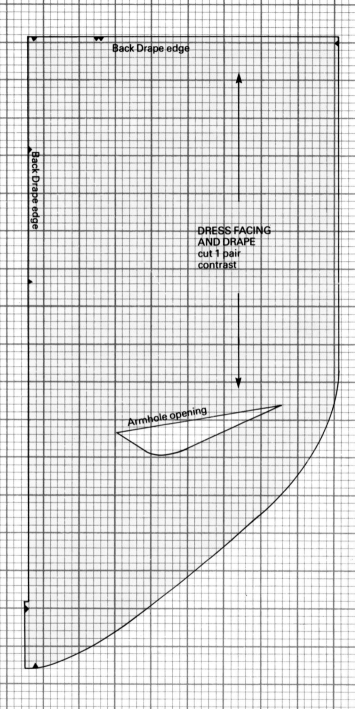

Back Drape edge

Back Drape edge

DRESS FACING
AND DRAPE
cut 1 pair
contrast

Armhole opening

For key to symbols see page nine

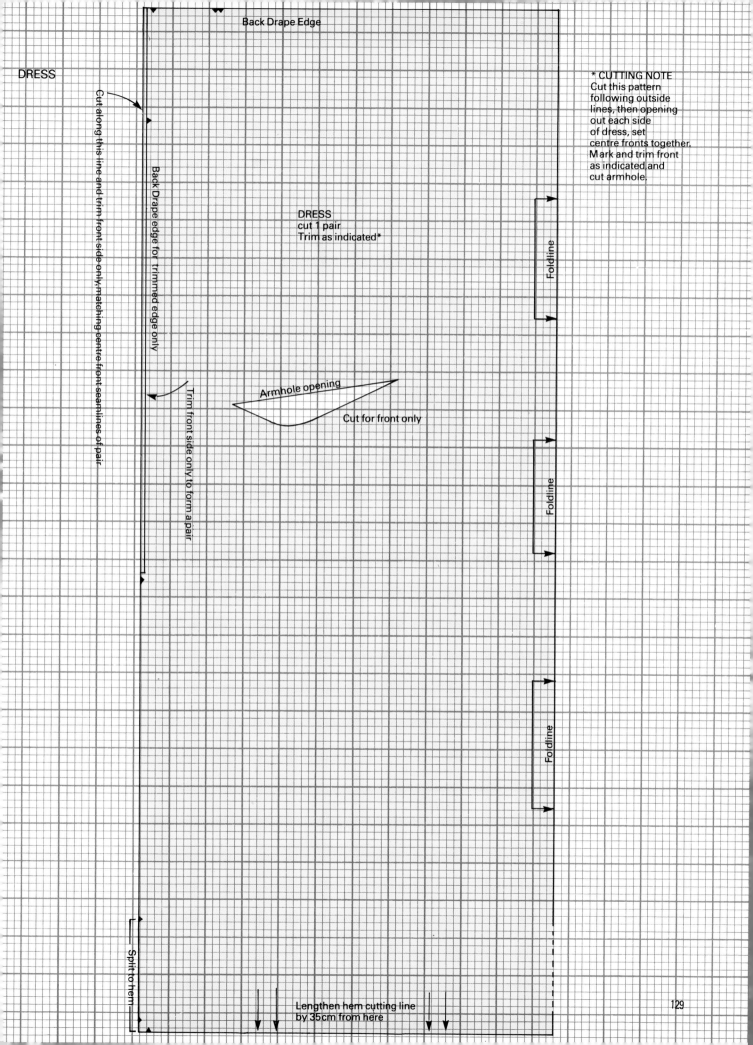

DRESS

Back Drape Edge

Cut along this line and trim front side only, matching centre front seamlines of pair

Back Drape edge for trimmed edge only

Trim front side only to form a pair

DRESS
cut 1 pair
Trim as indicated*

Armhole opening

Cut for front only

Foldline

Foldline

Foldline

* CUTTING NOTE
Cut this pattern
following outside
lines, then opening
out each side
of dress, set
centre fronts together.
Mark and trim front
as indicated and
cut armhole.

Split to hem

Lengthen hem cutting line
by 35cm from here

129

SHIRT

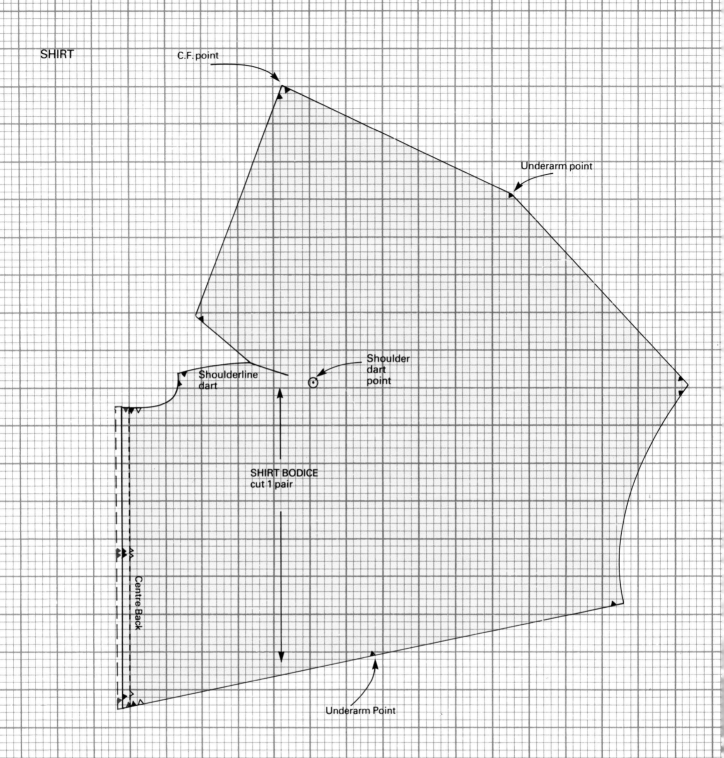

C.F. point

Underarm point

Shoulder
dart
point

Shoulderline
dart

SHIRT BODICE
cut 1 pair

Centre Back

Underarm Point

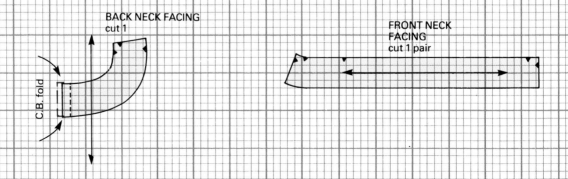

BACK NECK FACING
cut 1

C.B. fold

FRONT NECK
FACING
cut 1 pair

SHIRT

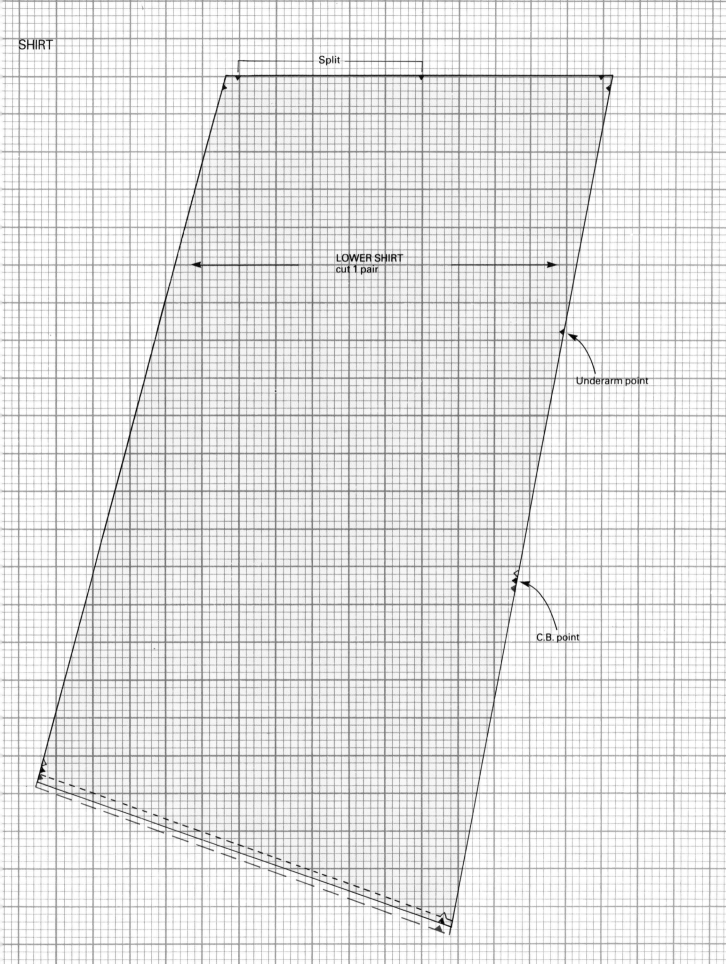

Split

LOWER SHIRT
cut 1 pair

Underarm point

C.B. point

131

VEST

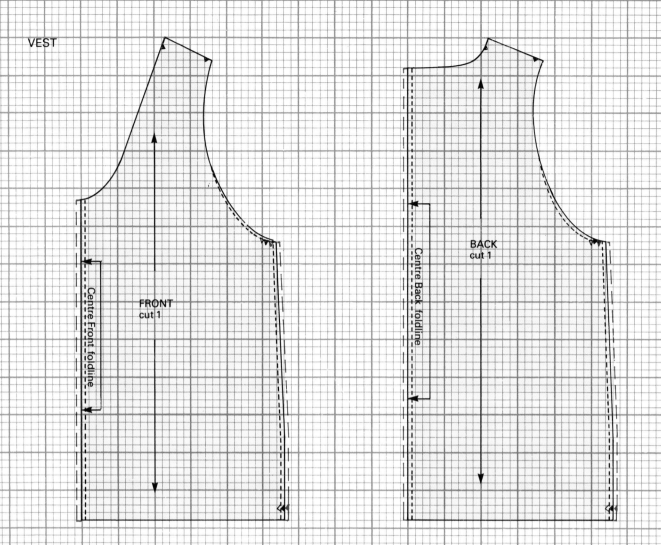

FRONT
cut 1

Centre Front foldline

BACK
cut 1

Centre Back foldline

SKIRT

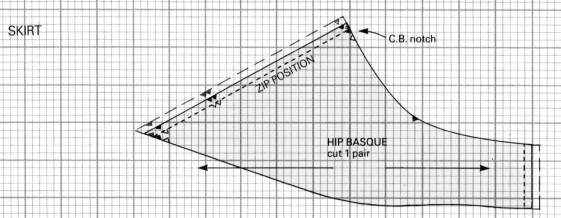

C.B. notch

ZIP POSITION

HIP BASQUE
cut 1 pair

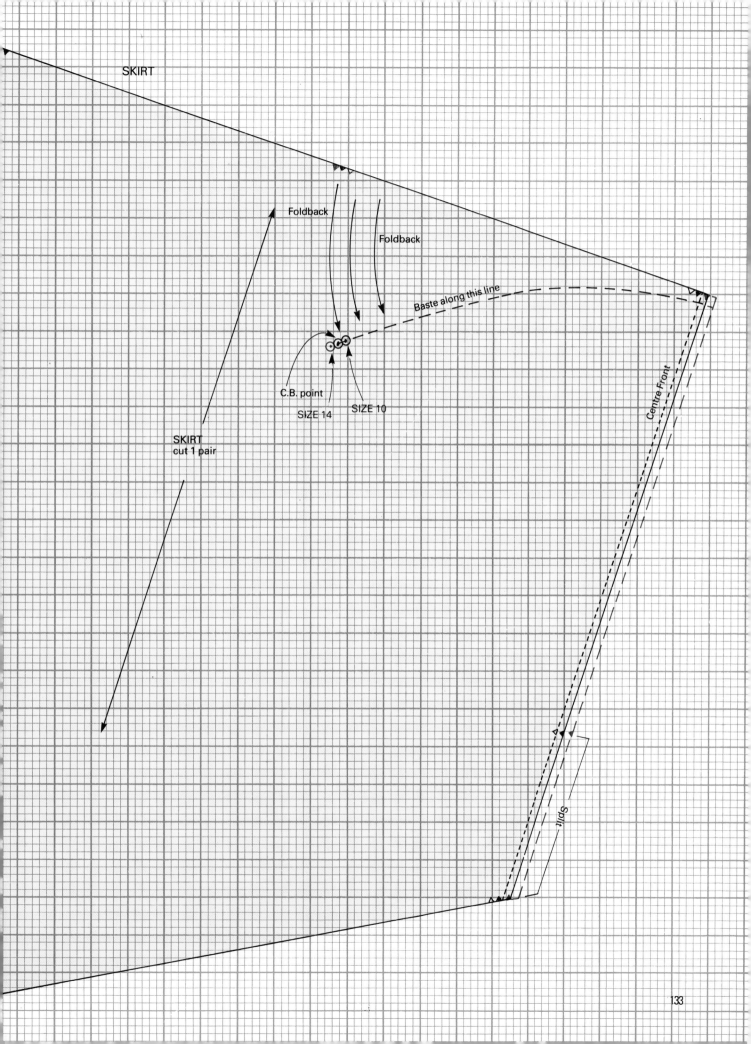

SKIRT

Foldback

Foldback

Baste along this line

C.B. point

SIZE 14

SIZE 10

Centre Front

SKIRT
cut 1 pair

Split

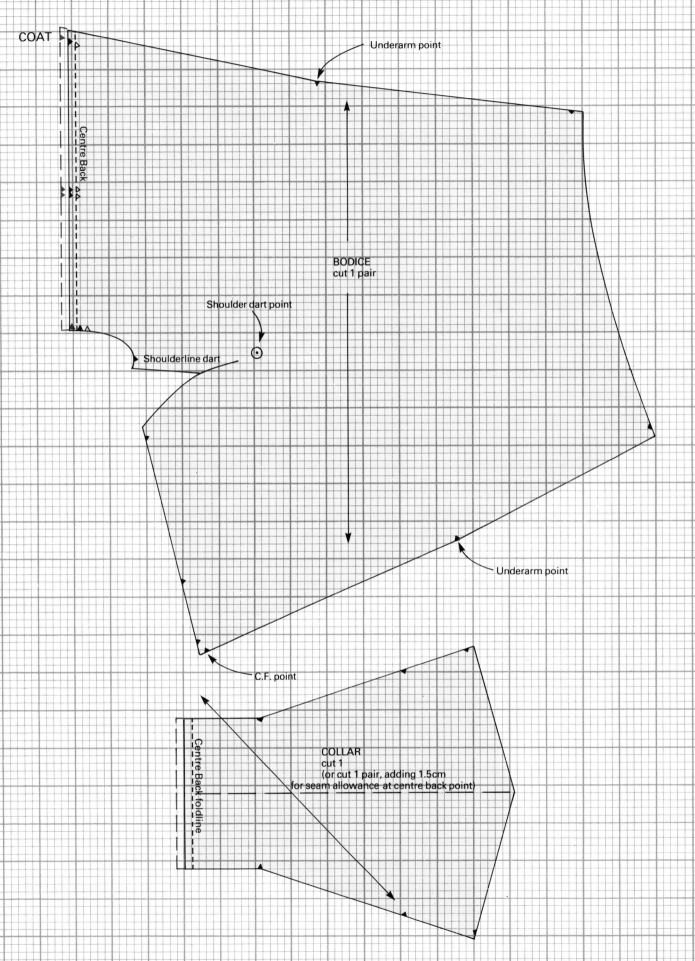

COAT

Underarm point

Centre Back

BODICE
cut 1 pair

Shoulder dart point

Shoulderline dart

Underarm point

C.F. point

Centre Back foldline

COLLAR
cut 1
(or cut 1 pair, adding 1.5cm
for seam allowance at centre back point)

COAT

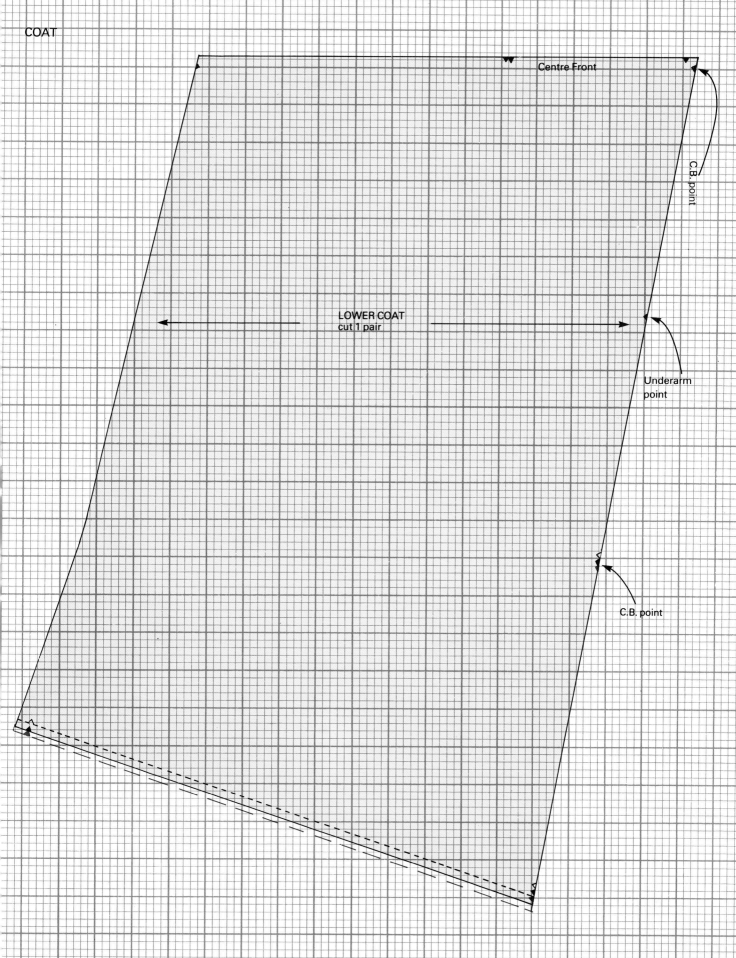

Centre Front

C.B. point

LOWER COAT
cut 1 pair

Underarm
point

C.B. point

Permutations

The pages that follow have been designed to show you how, by changing colour and fabric combinations, you can completely change the look of an outfit. By putting little cuttings of favourite fabrics against my sketches, you can play around with colour tones and balance, with weights and textures, until you find a combination which suits you. You can work with winter fabrics using shades of the same colour for sophisticated effect, and then lift the whole outfit or garment out of the ordinary by adding a bright flash of colour. Or you can play with textures, juxtaposing a ribbed wool coating with a smoother suiting and adding a wool challis printed in Paisley. Thereagain, work with blocks of bright, clashing colours for summer cottons, and yet another completely different effect is created. And if you combine more than one of these ideas, you will end up with a highly original and interesting set of garments. Remember, my ideas are simply here as a guideline; the real object is to give you a starting point. . . . .

Fine & Dandy

ABOVE A heavyweight, tweedy wool suiting, sophisticated and semi-classical, combines here with either of the two deeply toned velvets featured. I have added wool challis printed with abstract designs, flashed with purple, rust and sand, to brighten the dark tones and strengthen the overall effect. Use the tweed for the coat, skirt and waistcoat, and add velvet contrast panels to tie in with the soft wool blousing.

RIGHT A marvellous textured wool coating that works beautifully with an interesting, lighter-weight wool suiting woven in two colourways. Use the abstract designed lightweight wool for the blouse, or create a much younger, more fun, look with the check.

RIGHT Fabrics combined to show how the blouse and skirt may be made to look like a dress. Use the abstract-printed lightweight wool shown here, or dress it up using silk satin for the blouse and toning wool checks for the shirt.

Sports Chic

RIGHT Combine this strongly coloured, heavyweight tweedy wool coating with a lighterweight textured wool for the jacket and skirt, then pull the look together using one colour of wool for the knitted strips.

BELOW The use of pink, black and beige produces a totally different look. I have inset the pink rib knit for the coat with beige knitted strips, and then spiced the black wool jersey of the jacket, skirt and pants with the flowery wool weave shown here, in place of the knitted strips. The outfit is finally coordinated by adding knitted beige cuffs and ankle cuffs.

BOTTOM RIGHT As above for the coat, but using mauve knitted strips to coordinate with the printed needlecord.

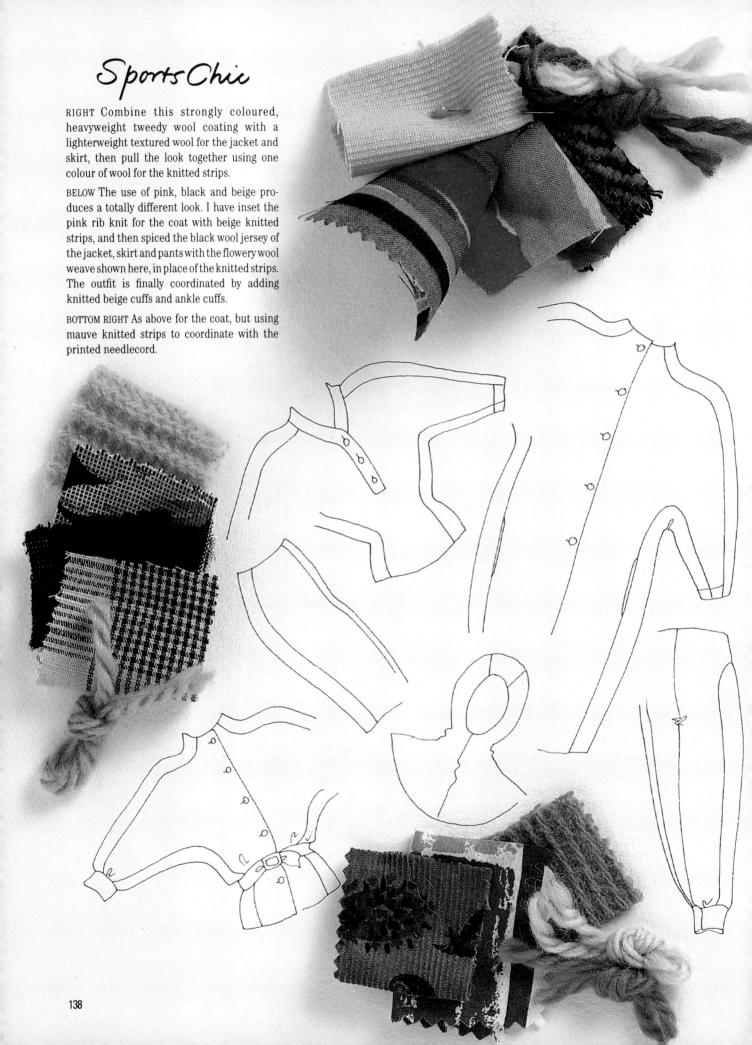

Country House

TOP LEFT Soft, thick tweedy coating combines with a lighterweight textured suiting which can be used for jacket, skirt and pants. Add a lightweight, brighter coloured printed wool for the shirt.

ABOVE A knobbly textured wool is used here for the suit. It is combined with a lighterweight woven or printed wool, which includes brighter colours, to 'lift' the blouse.

LEFT Dark navy blue wool coating would look wonderful used with the pure wool fake fur shown here for collar and cuffs. Add the blouse and pants in abstract printed wools, and aim for a very sophisticated and individual finish by inserting contrast print panels.

Streets Ahead

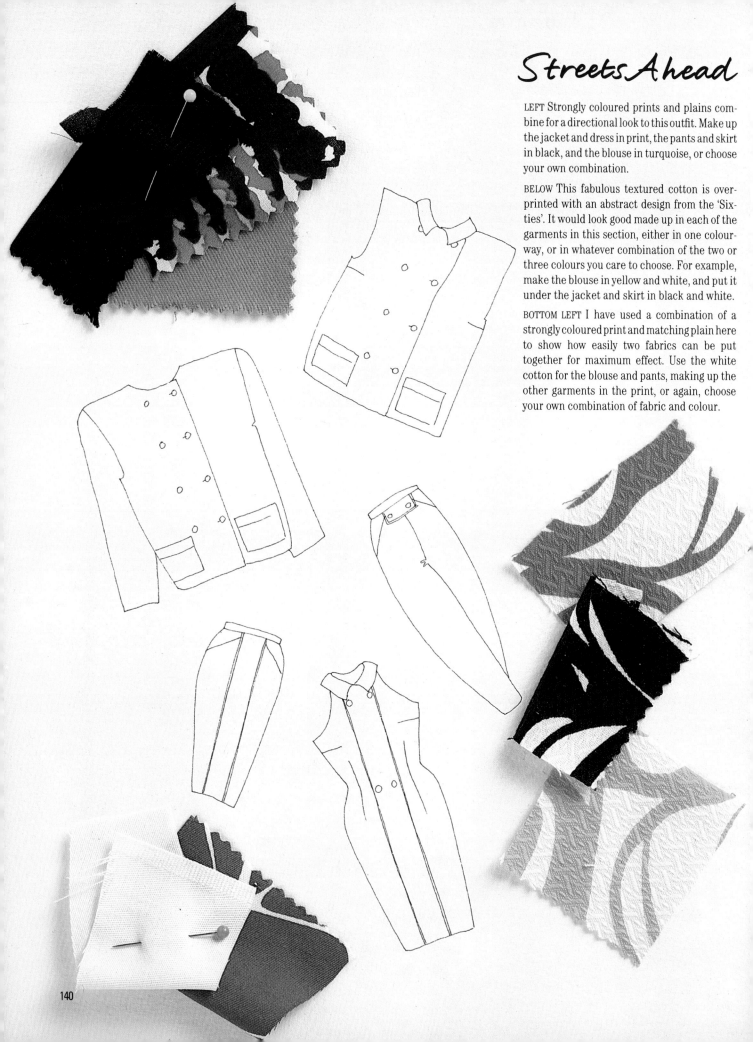

LEFT Strongly coloured prints and plains combine for a directional look to this outfit. Make up the jacket and dress in print, the pants and skirt in black, and the blouse in turquoise, or choose your own combination.

BELOW This fabulous textured cotton is overprinted with an abstract design from the 'Sixties'. It would look good made up in each of the garments in this section, either in one colourway, or in whatever combination of the two or three colours you care to choose. For example, make the blouse in yellow and white, and put it under the jacket and skirt in black and white.

BOTTOM LEFT I have used a combination of a strongly coloured print and matching plain here to show how easily two fabrics can be put together for maximum effect. Use the white cotton for the blouse and pants, making up the other garments in the print, or again, choose your own combination of fabric and colour.

Summer Breeze

TOP This whole outfit could be made up in these subdued but highly sophisticated stripes to beautiful effect. Use them in any combination you choose.

RIGHT Striped men's shirting gives a light, fresh, almost country feel to the outfit. Try contrasting hip basques using the narrow stripe on pants or skirt made in wider stripes; add a narrow striped waistcoat and vest, and wide striped ties.

RIGHT Brighter prints and plains change the mood completely. Use combinations of prints and plains, or go overboard and use the print exclusively. Try the skirt and duster coat in green damask-effect cotton, adding the little vest in yellow cotton for contrast.

Holiday Snaps

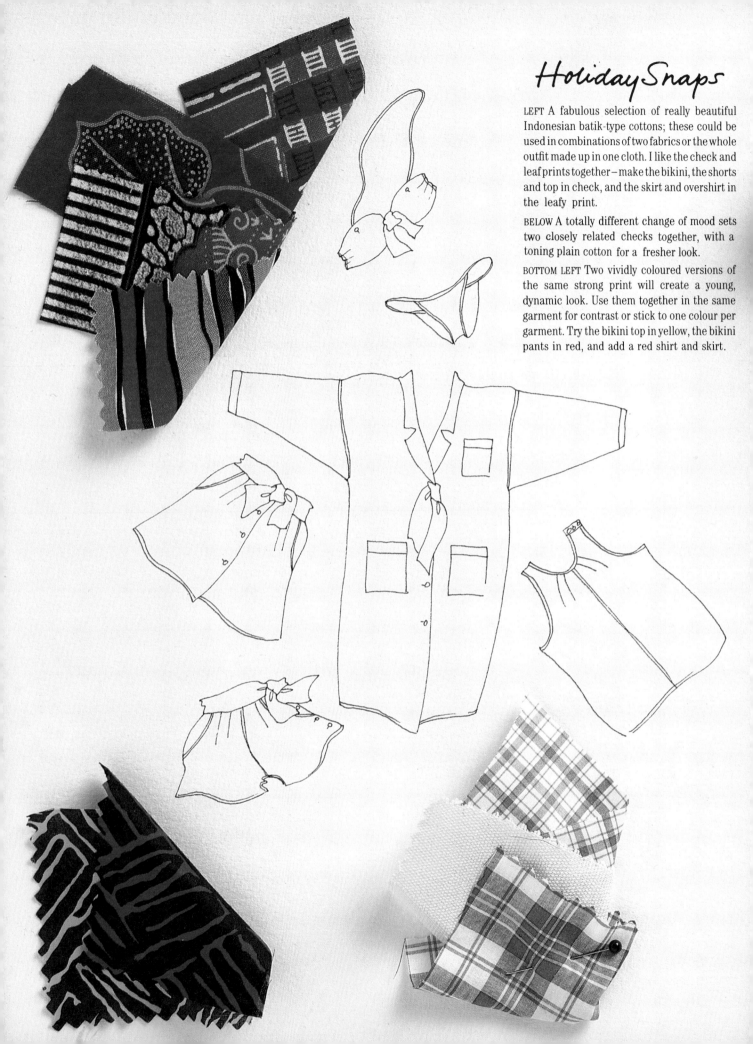

LEFT A fabulous selection of really beautiful Indonesian batik-type cottons; these could be used in combinations of two fabrics or the whole outfit made up in one cloth. I like the check and leaf prints together – make the bikini, the shorts and top in check, and the skirt and overshirt in the leafy print.

BELOW A totally different change of mood sets two closely related checks together, with a toning plain cotton for a fresher look.

BOTTOM LEFT Two vividly coloured versions of the same strong print will create a young, dynamic look. Use them together in the same garment for contrast or stick to one colour per garment. Try the bikini top in yellow, the bikini pants in red, and add a red shirt and skirt.

After Dark

ABOVE Soft wool challis printed with enormous abstract flowers, as shown in the main section, can look stunning. Simply make up into each of the garments using either one or both colour-ways for warm winter evenings.

TOP RIGHT Achieve an effect of delicate lingerie by combining pure silk satin with this lovely delicate silk faconne leaf print. Use the satin for the top and skirt, the silk for the blouse and coat. Very feminine, yet dressy. Wear with pumps and pants for important occasions.

RIGHT To create a stir! Wear a black silk satin skirt with a printed silk blouse that echoes the black base, using fabrics such as those shown here. Or make up the dress in printed satin, using the same print for contrast panels.

143

Special thanks…

My warm and grateful thanks go to all the people mentioned with whom I have so enjoyed working. In addition to those listed below, Ron Clark, Joan Clibbon, Christopher MacLehose, and Robin Wood, all at Collins. Klaus Zaan at Liberty. Mac Maclachlan and Ian Thorogood at Lewis's. Sheila Stewart at John Lewis's Partnership. Also Mary Parker, Rod Parker, Margaret Watkins, and my agent, Toby Eady.

Edited by Angela Jeffs

Designed by Graham Davis Associates
Designers: Graham Davis, Sarah Collins, Kevin Ryan

Fashion photography by Richard Lohr and Chris Roberts
Session organized by Polly Strettell
Hair by Paul Yacomine and Debbie Horgan at Daniel Galvin Colour Salon; Roger Hart at Joshua Galvin; Eugene at Trevor Sorbie
Make up by Debbie Bunn and Carol Langbridge
Models: Deanna Ashby, Kerry Boone, Denise Hill, Moira O'Brien and Emma Woollard, all from Bookings
Jewellery from Liberty; Rocks and Leading Lady at Grays Antique Market
Shoes by Midas

Pattern grading by Ron Klein

Pattern artwork by Andy Earl

Still life photography by Francis Lumley

Photograph of Charmian Watkins by John Clark

Sewing Machine Symphonie 300, kindly supplied by Singer Distribution Ltd

The fabrics used for each outfit are available as listed from the following stores:
Fine and Dandy – cavalry twill, furnishing velvet, moiré and silk organza from John Lewis Partnership
Sports Chic – pure wool jersey and knitting wool from Lewis's Ltd fashion fabric and knitting wool departments
Country House – dyeing by Chalfont Dyers
Summer Breeze – pure linen from Liberty
Holiday Snaps – Liberty Print tana lawn from Liberty
Streets Ahead – polycotton from Lewis's Ltd fashion fabric departments
After Dark – Liberty Print Varuna wool from Liberty; pure silk satin from the European Commission for the Promotion of Silk

All the fabrics displayed in 'Permutations' are from a selection available at Liberty.

Charmian Watkins runs a Designer Service for the benefit of home dressmakers who would like access to more of Charmian's patterns, and twice yearly fashion reports, which give advance information on trends for coming seasons.

If you would like details of the Charmian Watkins Designer Service, please send a stamped addressed envelope to Charmian Watkins Designer Service, 59 Temperley Road, London SW12 8QE for more information.